Adjust Your Sails

ADJUST YOUR SAILS

A Story of Navigating to a Life of Success

JOEL BROOKMAN

Copyright © 2012 by Joel Brookman

All rights reserved. No part of this book may be used or reproduced in any manner whatsoever without prior written consent of the publisher except in the case of brief quotations embodied in critical articles and reviews. Special book excerpts or customized printings can be created to fit specific needs.

For more information contact:
www.joelbrookman.com

ISBN: 978-0-9858747-5-9 (case bound book)
ISBN: 978-0-9858747-7-3 (ebook)

Printed in the United States of America

Book Design: Dotti Albertine

To my wife Stacy

Thank you for waking me up to understand existence beyond that which I was able to accept. Without your guidance and support this book would never exist.

To my children Sarah and Lori

Thank you for the inspiration. I wanted to create something that could provide guidance to you both throughout life. This accomplishment would serve as my greatest reward for writing this book.

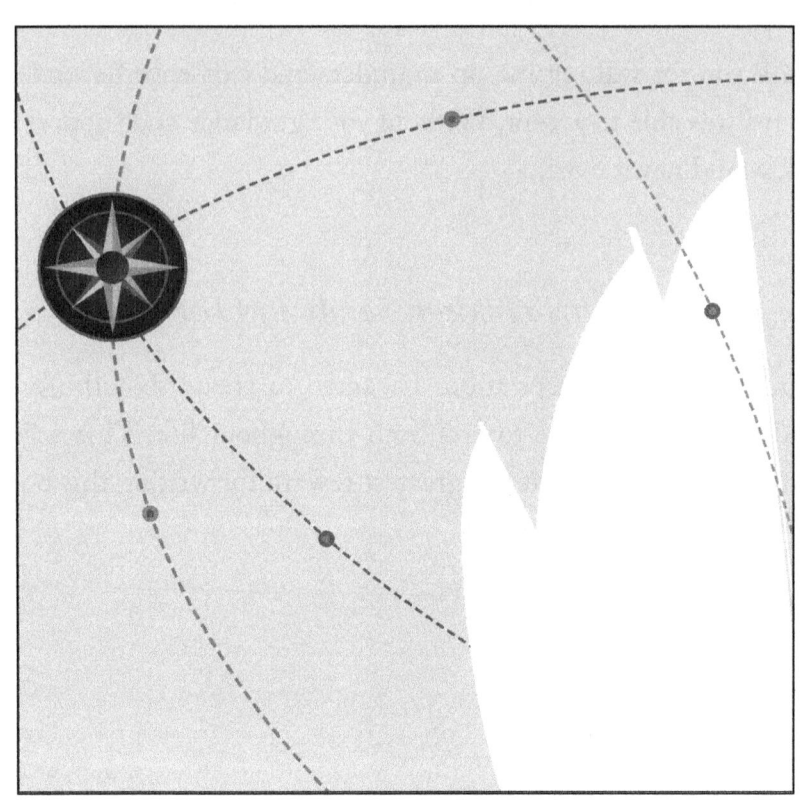

Acknowledgments

—To my parents Ellen and Bob: Thank you for encouraging me to accept that I could accomplish anything to which I set my mind. Your constant support has been among the greatest gifts of my life.

—To my brother Adam: Thank you for the advice and the many hours of your professional time that you contributed to this project.

—To my brother Marc: Thank you for your candid feedback and for lending your business prospective.

—To my coach and mentor Joan King: Without your guidance, the production of this book would have occurred years in the future and its outcome, far different.

—To my friend Martin Sokol: Thanks for being a great sounding board and for providing literary direction.

—To Dr. Ed Taub: Many thanks for your technical assistance.

—Thanks to Scott Menaul for his amazing artistic work on the cover.

—For all my mentors in business: You helped me reach a place professionally that has given me the opportunity to do what I love, provided a wonderful lifestyle for my family and given me tremendous insight in business and in life.

—To you (the reader): Thank you for taking time to read this book. If you implement one idea that positively impacts your life as a result, then I will deem my endeavor as a success.

Prologue

I came to the realization many years ago that I was making my life much more difficult than it needed to be. I was swimming against the current instead of using it to get where I wanted to go. After years of struggle, I finally learned that there are some basic concepts that, if followed, can improve one's entire life experience. I only wish I had been introduced to these principles earlier.

Growing up, I never knew exactly what I wanted to do. The only thing I was clear about is that I wanted to make a lot of money. When I finished college, I set a goal for myself to become a millionaire by age 30. I became consumed with this goal. I started a property maintenance/construction company to accomplish it. The business was building nicely within a very short time. I began taking on bigger jobs and growing my staff. At its peak, I had about 20 employees.

I got myself (my ego) so wrapped up in the business that it began to define who I thought I was. The challenge grew as I became reliant on other people, who in many cases, would not follow through. I began to worry about them not showing up on jobs. I worried about cost overruns, and ultimately, I worried about my business failing.

Ironically, things were actually going quite well at the time, though I couldn't see that. I had a constant fear of what could go wrong. The stress that came as a result of fearing failure became so consuming that I would get out of bed three days a week at 5:00 a.m. and literally head straight to the bathroom to throw up. I had focused all my energy on **not failing**—and the stress began taking its toll on my body.

My lesson from years of running my business that way is that if you focus your energy consistently on an outcome, you will actually bring it into being.

That is exactly what happened to me in the end. My business ultimately fell apart as I worried right past it. The amazing part is that I couldn't even admit to myself that I had failed. To top things off, as the business (my entire world, as I comprehended it) was falling apart, my marriage of two years was disintegrating as well.

Soon after the marriage ended and the business dissolved, I decided on a complete life change. I had gone to school for finance and had some contacts in the money management industry. I was lucky enough to land a job at a top money management firm in Boston. There is nothing better than being young, single, and living in Boston except possibly being young, single, wealthy, and living in Boston. At that point wealth was definitely not part of the equation. My biggest challenge was figuring out where I was going out every night. My biggest expense was bar bills, racked up through my relentless pursuit of the almighty female.

My new job began with an intense education on the financial markets, specifically how they pertained to the world of asset management. Once you were up to speed technically, the proving ground began. If you paid your dues and excelled, bigger things could happen. And they did. One day, after my second year with the firm, my boss's boss asked me if I would prefer to run Mutual Fund distribution for New York City or Florida. I chose New York. Two months later I was living on the beach in Florida. So much for my boss accepting my input.

This new job was all about building long-term relationships with the most successful financial advisors in Florida. I began to become very interested in what made certain people more successful than others within the same industry. This study became my passion, which I continue to this day (16 years as of this writing). During this same period, I began to read every book on personal growth and success I could get my hands on.

What I discovered is that, on the surface, there were no detectable common traits among successful people. Sure they all worked hard, but they all seemed to achieve success through different means. As I began to dig deeper though, I found that there were some commonalities, but they were not detectable from the conversations I was having. Most people were not consciously aware of what they were doing to bring success about. It eventually brought me to examine how they think as opposed to what they say.

One characteristic I quickly discovered is that before virtually every one of these people was ever successful, they inherently knew and had no doubt that it would happen. They approached situations with their desired outcome in mind. The key, I began to discover, was to start from the end and work backwards. In other words, approach any task with the desired outcome in mind.

The biggest catalyst to positive change in my life came from my current wife, Stacy. She introduced me to a completely new way of looking at life. It began with the study of how things work universally. By this, I mean that she seemed to understand what I will call the technology of the universe, and the extent of what we as humans are capable of accomplishing.

Through the immersion in quantum physics and personal growth, combined with my obsession of uncovering the drivers of success, a picture began to come together. Today I am a happily married father of two wonderful little girls. I have an amazing extended family, an incredibly supportive array of friends, many of whom go back to my early childhood. I am fortunate to have the financial wherewithal combined with a supportive spouse that allow me to follow my passions in life. Those passions include travel, rock 'n' roll, and skiing.

I am absolutely convinced that my life situation would not have developed as it has without the insights I have gained over the last 15 years. I am fortunate to have worked my way into a terrific career with one of the world's top asset management firms. To date, I have achieved every career goal I have set for myself and have become a senior executive in the area of corporate development for a leading Wall Street firm. I am one of the lucky few who actually look forward to going to work every day. Each day is completely different and presents new challenges. I currently live in Palm Beach, Florida and spend every possible moment in my second home in Vail, Colorado.

At the end of the day, though, I am still a pretty simple guy. The difference between me now and the guy that was throwing up from stress three days a week is that I have woken up to see how things work universally. I have integrated these concepts into my life—and now I want to share them with others. I want others to enjoy the same success and personal happiness that I have been able to achieve.

If you are wondering if it's possible for you to have the type of life I now have, the answer is YES. I am absolutely convinced that through discipline and subtle redirection of one's thoughts, anyone can absolutely, positively create the life they want to live. There are many wonderful books out there that cover some of the same concepts I will be discussing. I have sifted through a tremendous number of these books and, combined with my own experiences and ideas, I have created what I believe to be a concise, impactful primer that anyone can read and learn from. My goal has been to provide a balanced approach that speaks to "regular" people who may not be familiar with these life-changing concepts, as well as to depict a straightforward and actionable path to success for those who have been exposed to this information but have yet to incorporate it into their life.

Ultimately, I am trying to create a mainstream book that identifies the factors that contribute to the success of the most advanced among us. You will work on concepts like:

- Articulating your life's desires.
- Absorbing knowledge about the creation process.
- The powerful combination of action and discipline.
- Building knowledge-based ritualized activities to capture and fulfill your desires.
- The steps associated with making your desires a reality.

Note that nothing you read in this book will be difficult to accomplish, yet nothing is easy. Practicing and implementing what I will share with you does not need to be time consuming, but it will be if you choose it to be so. The concepts are very straightforward and the work involved is not complicated. But you need to absorb the concepts and keep doing the work continuously. Discipline is one of the most important factors toward achievement.

While I recognize that most of us don't live in a monastery or meditate eight hours a day, the issue is, how do we take the principles that the most evolved people among us live by and apply them to our lives as they do? After all, we still have to deal with our work environment, take care of our families, and live the so-called rat race. But if the rat took a few minutes every day to step off the wheel, he would probably see things in a much different prospective.

For that reason, I have aimed to make this book as easy to assimilate as possible. As I read the seemingly endless array of personal development books in preparation for this writing, I realized that for the vast majority of them, I had a difficult time staying engaged. I decided that I needed a way to not only keep the reader interested in the subject matter, but I also needed to attract people who would not normally be open to these types of books. I attempted to accomplish this by building a story and then creating the personal development ideas within the confines of the story.

We have all read books that inspired us. Most often we grasp the power of the text as we read them. Despite our greatest intentions, within a short period of time we resume life as usual, ultimately failing to integrate the material that inspired us into our daily life. My challenge for the reader in creating the action steps is to get you to act on the inspiration you feel. At the end of each chapter in the second part of the book, you will see a series of action steps. If you are inspired by the message and decide to make the commitment to change, follow the steps. These steps are aimed at helping you integrate the subject matter into your daily life. Think of each action step as a way for you to integrate a particular concept into your life. The goal of the action steps are to provide you with routines to follow that can maximize your chance of success in a particular area.

Some of you may not wish to begin doing the action steps initially. Many people prefer to read the entire book first without interruption. If that applies to you, go ahead and read the book all the way through, but then go back and review and do those exercises that are beneficial to you. You can also come back to this material periodically as a means to continually stay on the path toward creating that desired life situation.

I hope that these ideas will wake you up to how life works universally and provide you not only with the tools to create your desired life situation but also the mechanics of how to make them work for you. My wish is that this book gives you a practical path toward directing your life toward your desires. If you do all I set forth in this book, you will, at the minimum, create a blueprint toward achieving your desired life situation. So I invite you to sit back with an open mind and begin designing the life you desire.

—Joel Brookman

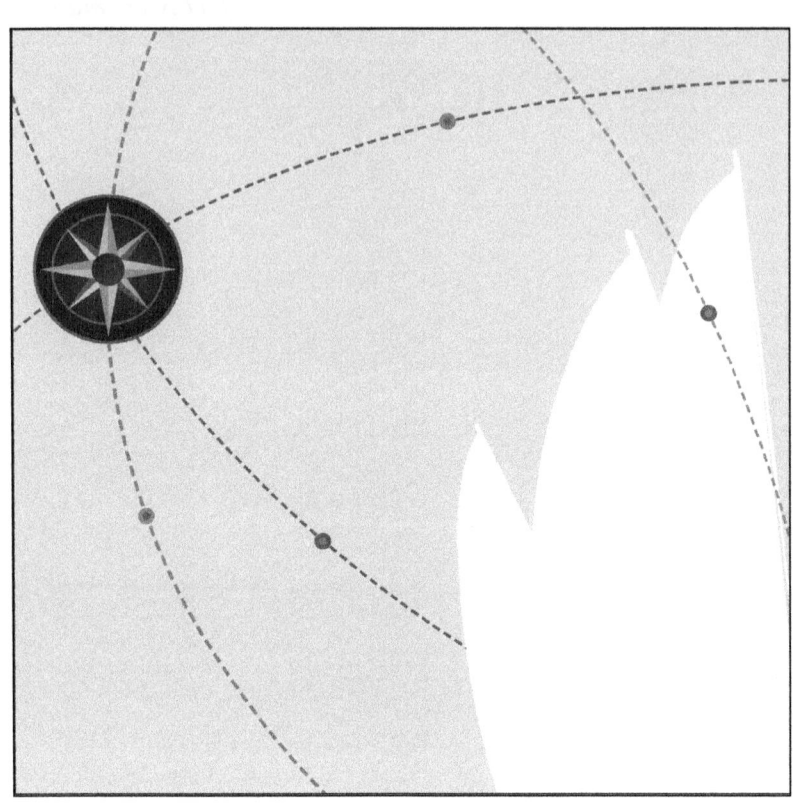

Chapter 1

EVERYBODY CALLED EDWARD NOONAN, Jr. the luckiest guy in the world.

If he wasn't the absolute luckiest, he came pretty close. Eddie, as he was affectionately called, had about as great a job as anyone could hope for—he ran $850 million of the $20 billion dollar asset base for a money management firm called The Forecastle Group. Forecastle was one of Boston's most successful privately held companies. The firm was based in Back Bay. Eddie's office had a spectacular, wrap-around view that included the Charles River, Cambridge, and to the west, Fenway Park. His office was steps from his condo, a Newbury Street triplex that had been featured in all the architectural magazines. His live-in, a lingerie model at Louis of Boston, the most elegant store in the city, also had a five-minute walk to work.

Perhaps Eddie's greatest stroke of luck was that he got to work for his father, Ned Noonan, the legendary founder of The Forecastle Group. Everyone in the financial community of Boston knew his story. Ned had grown up in a small village in Ireland, raised by his father after his mother died during childbirth. His father sought refuge in a bottle and in short order, assumed the role of the town drunk. The neighbors actually took up a collection for Ned to sail to the United States, partly to get away from his father and partly because his math skills were renowned throughout the county. Everyone figured that Ned would go to Harvard or MIT and become a math professor.

Instead, he graduated first in his class at Harvard, and first in his MBA class at Wharton. Theoretical aspects of mathematics didn't interest him nearly as much as making money, and he made tons of it. Ned and his wife, Helen, had raised Eddie in baronial splendor in a house built to look like a castle on Marblehead Neck. The family belonged to both of the best yacht clubs in Marblehead, and Eddie grew up on the water.

During the summer, it was said that Marblehead Harbor was so packed with boats that you could step from one to the next and cross from the lighthouse at the tip of Marblehead Neck all the way back to Old Town without getting your feet wet. A 65-foot schooner belonging to Ned, the *Maximum Liquidity*, was one of the biggest boats in the Harbor.

Eddie followed in his father's footsteps and attended both Harvard and Wharton, although he didn't have his father's illustrious record in either school. To be frank, he didn't have the motivation, although he certainly had a lot more fun than his father. To be fair to Eddie, it was hard to concentrate on studies when, thanks to his father's fame and connections, the city was at his feet—the best seats for any Red Sox, Celtics, or Patriots game; the best table at any top restaurant in Boston, and of course, the *Maximum Liquidity*, which was always available during the summer months because Ned took so little time off from work.

And then one day in 2007, Ned made the decision that would change everything. He was going to sail to Ireland on his boat, with his son, whom everyone acknowledged as one of the finest sailors on the North Shore. He would retrace and reverse the voyage that had brought him to the United States, to fame, and to fortune. And he would do it with the confidence in the ability to handle any challenge because, after all, Ned was very competent and Eddie was a truly gifted sailor.

At the last minute, Eddie bailed. His model girlfriend booked a shoot in Antigua, and Eddie decided to go along, in part to be with her and in part to keep the photographers from hitting on her after (or even during) the shoots.

There was no question of the seaworthiness of the vessel or the will of its owner. The only question was whether he had the requisite sailing experience—occasional weekend jaunts off Marblehead Harbor hardly qualified even someone as certain of his own destiny as Ned to sail the Atlantic. Ned's wife, Helen, counseled him not to make the crossing alone. After much thought, Ned decided to go on without his son, and he set sail in early spring for a voyage that was supposed to take three weeks. If the weather had cooperated, Ned Noonan might have made it to Ireland. Unfortunately, one last winter storm churned the waters off Newfoundland as Ned passed by, swamping the boat in 10-foot swells. Ned's body was never recovered.

The *Maximum Liquidity* eventually found its way to a deserted beach on the Newfoundland coast, where it was discovered by a couple on a quiet walk. It was towed back to a boat-building shop in Newburyport, Massachusetts, up the coast from Marblehead, with a reputation for repairing boats that had undergone disastrous wrecks.

And suddenly, Eddie was thrust into even greater prominence, no longer responsible for just a portion of Forecastle's assets, but the entire asset base and the firm itself.

Edward Noonan, Jr., the sudden loss of his father notwithstanding, might have been the luckiest guy in the world, but the one thing he lacked was confidence in his own decision-making abilities. Whenever he traded, he relied on the expertise of his Harvard and Wharton classmates, who had gone on to prominent positions in Wall Street's top investment banks. Their advice might have been slightly self-serving, but it was usually on the mark. The combination of that guidance along with a strong market had given Eddie great results, but never the absolute security that he was succeeding on his own. There was always a slight hollowness to his victories, because he had the self-awareness to recognize that if he hadn't been born to the right father, he would never have been this successful. He knew in his heart that luck had played a huge role in every aspect of his life. As long as his father was running the firm, he was content to sit back and run his financial stocks. Those who worked closely with him running money were convinced he had been very lucky. Now, he had to be more than lucky. He had to be good.

The problem was that he wasn't. He kept his own office, instead of moving into his father's, which remained untouched and unchanged. But that was pretty much the only thing that stayed the same in Eddie's life, now that he was running The Forecastle Group. His father had adhered to a philosophy of steady, conservative growth, which had resulted in security and even serenity for the firm's many clients. Because of its stability and long-term success, The Forecastle Group was the investment vehicle of choice for many of the downtown law and accounting firms that represented Boston's wealth, old and new. Ned hadn't just built wealth; he had built trust. Eddie now felt a responsibility to make his own mark on the business.

The market had been on an improbable tear for years. The easy money of the post-9/11 era had led to vast creation of wealth in both real estate and equities, so there was more and more money flooding into the market, pushing the Dow ever higher. When the Dow reached 12,000, 15,000 was suddenly in sight. And predictions of the Dow reaching 20,000 were written by some respected economists and analysts who made irresistible cases for such vertigo-inducing growth.

Something inside Eddie rejected the possibility of Dow 20,000, but he, like everyone else, wanted to believe. He could still hear his father repeating his favorite maxims, "Trees don't grow to the sky" and "They don't ring a bell at the top." Indeed, Eddie's intuition told him that, for one reason or another, the run-up was done and it was time to take money off the table. But he was not the kind of person to make his reputation on caution—that was his father's legacy. He wanted to be known as a game-changer.

So Eddie set his intuition aside and solicited the advice of his Harvard and Wharton classmates yet again. They told him exactly what he wanted to hear—that the future for equities was bright—that things would be different this time. They told him that no one in his or her right mind would jump off the train right now. If the Dow does go to 20,000, or even a measly 15,000, would you want to be the guy on the outside with his face pressed to the window? How severely would Jim Kramer or the rest of the TV talking heads be trashing Eddie? Was that any way to treat a legacy of his father's success?

"So what do I do?" Eddie asked.

"Invest in us," came the siren song from his Wall Street friends. "Buy any big investment bank on Wall Street you can get your hands on. Trees may not grow to the sky, but have you ever visited a redwood grove? That's high enough, isn't it?" He resisted at first, but as those stocks pulled back in what he viewed as a correction, he began to see great value. At 20 percent off he jumped in with both feet. He became so convinced that he was right, he began to use leverage. For every dollar that went in, three went to work. Thirty-five percent of his allocation was to financials.

Eddie did something his father would never have dreamt of doing. He made a huge bet on financials, with the majority weighted toward investment banks. The move unbalanced all the portfolios of The Forecastle Group, as others at the firm whispered to each other (but not to Eddie). These banks have been around forever, Eddie reasoned. Even if there is a downturn, they're all about allocating capital. They'll know what to do. My downside is protected and my upside is unlimited.

But instead of going up, the market continued to drop, pulling the financial stocks down another 30 percent from where he had started buying them. It didn't take a financial analyst to figure out these numbers. He had lost everything—for his clients, for his friends, and for his family. If they had all their money with him (and close to half did), they were broke.

The Forecastle Group ended up making a very, very big bet on the shares of some great financial institutions that, as fate would have it, had but months to live. The year 2008 arrived, and with it the economic collapse, which took down not only the banking houses like Lehman Brothers but also all those who had invested in them.

Like The Forecastle Group.

By 2009, just eighteen months under the direction of Eddie Noonan, Jr., The Forecastle Group was bankrupt.

It was the biggest investment shock in Boston in decades. This hit the heart of Boston. Forecastle's clients were the people that controlled the city. They were the wealth; they drove Boston's economy.

Edward Noonan, Jr., who had told himself and anyone who would listen, "It's always better to be lucky than good," was suddenly neither.

It got worse. His personal fortune, and the money that Ned had left Helen, had all been invested with The Forecastle Group. Now it was all gone. Eddie's Back Bay triplex was also owned by The Forecastle Group, not outright by Eddie, which meant that creditors got it and couldn't get him out fast enough. Even the castle on Marblehead Neck belonged to The Forecastle Group, which meant that it, too, went under the hammer in a bankruptcy auction, forcing Helen out of the home where she and Ned had lived for 20 years.

And when the money disappeared, so did his girlfriend. Eddie had gone from the top of the world to a situation for which he had no training or preparation. Even his classmates from Harvard and Wharton couldn't help him now. Who in finance would even think of hiring the son of the owner of The Forecastle Group, now mocked as The Foreclosure Group?

The only thing Eddie owned outright, as it happened, was the boat, the 65-foot schooner called the *Maximum Liquidity*, restored to pristine condition, bobbing gently in the waters of Newburyport Harbor. Since The Forecastle Group didn't own it, Eddie still did. He might not have had the money to keep up with marina fees, but out of respect for Ned, the boat was allowed to keep its place in Newburyport Harbor.

Eddie went back to Marblehead, where he rented a room in a house in Old Town and where he got a job tending bar at Maddie's, the name by which locals knew a bar half a block from the harbor. The bar's real name was the Sail Loft, but no one called it that. Eddie took his lunches and dinners at the restaurant upstairs and poured the 16-ounce mixed drinks for which Maddie's was justifiably famous. He avoided the yacht clubs, where his memberships had lapsed anyway, since they were paid for by The Forecastle Group. The last thing he wanted to do was run into anyone whose money he had lost. He would lower his eyes and all but duck under the bar whenever anyone from his past life as an investment professional entered Maddie's.

And then one day his landlord told him that the house where he was renting a room was about to be sold, and Eddie had to be out by the first of the month.

No job, no girlfriend, no money, no relationship with his mother, who had not forgiven him for losing all her money as well as destroying the family firm, no options.

He only had two things left in life. One was the 65-foot yacht, bobbing on the water in Newburyport, twenty minutes north of Marblehead. The other was a shaggy but amiable black lab mix that began following Eddie around after he left the bar. The wait staff had looked after the dog for years, but the dog had a special affinity for Eddie. They were two lost souls, simply scraping by with no real home.

For Edward Noonan, Jr., it was a no-brainer.

It was time to get away.

And not just anywhere. One night, behind the bar, his destination became obvious. He wanted to complete the journey his father never could, sailing solo to Ireland. The trip he should have taken with his father. The trip for which he was wracked with guilt—maybe if he had been on board, he might have been able to keep his father alive.

Once in Ireland, he could sell the boat, live cheaply, maybe tend bar somewhere, and figure out what exactly he was going to do with the rest of his life.

Eddie made up his mind.

He was going to sail to Ireland.

Chapter 2

IT JUST WASN'T FAIR.

Kathy Drucker had done everything right—good grades in college, great scores on the LSAT, three years in the top ten percent of her class at Boston College Law School, president of Law Review, and a standout summer associate at the downtown Boston law firm of Sykes & Martland.

And then came the economic collapse of 2008, affecting pretty much everything to do with real estate not just in Boston but across the country, and with it, the law firm of Sykes & Martland. The firm primarily dealt in real estate development, which Kathy had identified back in college as the most reasonable form of law that she could practice. It was transactional, which meant that you did deals instead of trying cases in court. Except for the occasional all-nighters when major deals were closing, you got in at a reasonable hour, you left at a reasonable hour, and nobody needed you nights and weekends. Not like litigation, where you were working around the clock when you were preparing for a trial and working even longer hours when you were in court. And now, all of a sudden, the bottom had dropped out of the real estate market.

Nobody was lending. Nobody was building. Nobody was doing

anything. Which meant that Sykes & Martland simply didn't need any additional lawyers, and they wouldn't for the foreseeable future.

So here sat Kathy, in her share of a rent-controlled, semi-squalid apartment just off Comm Ave. She lived close to the B train on the Green Line that had taken her either east to law school or west to the downtown offices of Sykes, where she had worked part-time and summers since the conclusion of her first year of law school. Her life had been pretty much governed by the B line for the last three years. And now, here she was, facing a mountain of college and law school debt, re-reading the letter from her former employer over and over again, hoping that each time she read it, it might be a little different from the previous time.

But it wasn't.

"We regret to inform you," the letter began, "that due to changes in the economy, we will no longer be able to offer you a position." It ended, "Very truly yours," whatever that meant.

It was amazing to Kathy just how few words it took for her entire future to go up in flames.

If Sykes was laying off lawyers, so were all the other firms. Kathy knew then that her chances of finding another job were zero to none. B.C. was a highly regarded, and super expensive, law school, but it wasn't Harvard. And even Harvard 3Ls were encountering the same crash of the legal economy that faced Kathy.

A ton of debt, no prospects in her field, and no idea of what to do next.

No boyfriend, either, for that matter. Law school, and particularly Law Review, had sucked all the time out of her life for anything like a serious social life. Idly, she went on Match.com and set her parameters for guys within five years of her age who live within 40 miles of Boston. While reading through the profiles, she came across the name of a town she had never heard of, growing up as she had in the Midwest.

It was called Newburyport.

She liked the sound of the name and switched from Match.com to Google Images, where she studied, and quickly fell in love with, the nineteenth century red brick buildings of the area nearest the harbor and the water itself. All those boats in the harbor. It looked like freedom. More importantly, it looked nothing like Comm Ave., with its endless traffic and the endless waits for the B line that was supposed to be taking her not just to law school and the office of Sykes & Martland, but to a better life.

From Google Images she went to Craigslist and quickly found three opportunities for apartments to share in and around Newburyport Harbor. She borrowed a friend's car, an old, rusting Volvo beater that had somehow survived an unknowable number of Boston winters, and drove up to Newburyport, getting incredibly lost on the tangle of roads that led from 93 into the town. She looked at all three units and settled on the third, a share of a two-bedroom condo a few blocks from the waterfront with a girl her age who didn't smoke and who worked at the marina and thought that she might be able to get Kathy a job there as well.

Kathy drove back to Boston, loaded all of her stuff in her friend's car, leaving behind her law school textbooks and anything to do with what would have been her legal career, and moved in that same day.

As it turned out, Kathy couldn't get a job at the marina, but she was able to find work, waiting tables in a restaurant nearby. The only problem was that the amount of money she made from her waitressing job didn't quite cover her living expenses and the interest on her student loans, which were now seriously in arrears. She fell a couple of months behind in her rent, which was so foreign to Kathy's thrifty Midwestern nature that she couldn't stand it. She came home one night to an eviction note and a shiny new deadbolt on the front door. Her roommate had at least taken the privilege of shoving all of her things into one big suitcase and cardboard boxes. Everything she owned suddenly looked so trivial in front of the door.

That night, she did something she couldn't imagine ever doing.

Too embarrassed to tell the truth, she went back to Boston, borrowed her friend's Volvo, and slept in it.

In an alley, just off Comm Ave.

It was the longest night of her life.

The next day, she dropped off the car keys at her friend's place and took the train back to Newburyport and did something she also never imagined she would have done. She got the idea from an article she had read in the local newspaper.

She broke into one of the boats in the harbor, and slept in it.

It was a huge boat, maybe the biggest she'd ever seen. Of course, coming from the Midwest, she didn't have much of a frame of reference for yachts. All she knew was that if you waited until around 11 p.m., when the cops were sitting in their own cars, sleeping or trying to keep warm, you could sneak into practically any boat in the harbor. And as long as you were out by about five the next morning, you'd be fine.

You could even leave stuff on a boat and find it there the next day. You could shower or do whatever you needed to do. A lot of them had fully stocked kitchens and bars. Kathy had heard that 95 percent of the boats never left the harbor, and that in most cases, the boats sat idle from the time they were moved from dry dock in the spring 'til the time they were taken out of the water in the fall. And of the others, in only a few cases did the owners even come down on the weekends to sit on the deck and have a few drinks.

Kathy soon found herself part of a small community of people around her age who were living on boats. Once you had moved onto one, people tended to respect your "homesteading," so you were okay. What attracted Kathy to this one particular boat was not its size but its name. *Maximum Liquidity*. She just thought it sounded cool, and since she was about as illiquid as one could be, it seemed like the right boat for her.

She had been living on the boat for about three or four months, walking to her restaurant job, and hoping not to get caught. As for the student loans, well, maybe she'd get caught up with them at some point, but certainly this wasn't the time. And since it was very hard for collection agencies to find somebody living on a boat, she figured she would be okay for the time being. The hard thing was actually getting to sleep. The idea that anyone could find her, and maybe have her arrested, or that something bad could happen, was never far from her mind. That's why they created Ambien, she told herself, and a couple of pills later, she would be deeply asleep.

One night, she came back to the boat and saw that someone had been on board. Somebody had dropped off a few suitcases and had completely restocked the refrigerator. There was also a set of maps and charts on the dining room table. Kathy had never seen charts before, so she didn't know quite what to make of them. But she could read, and she saw that they covered the North Atlantic.

That's interesting, she thought. She took all of her stuff that had been lying around the captain's cabin below deck—the ship slept a half-dozen—and put them neatly away in a closet beneath the California king-size bed.

When she came back that night, she got on board and stepped carefully over a new set of sails lying on the deck. She made a mental note to start looking for a new boat in the morning. This one was obviously going places.

She was asleep by midnight with the alarm on her phone set to wake her at the usual hour, 5 a.m. Getting only five hours of sleep was getting old, but it was better than sleeping in a car. At that time, she could also scan the marina for unoccupied boats.

The next morning, she arose in a panic. Her cell phone battery must have died during the night, because it didn't wake her. On top of that, the boat seemed to be rocking.

She blinked a couple of times and stared out a porthole.

She wasn't in Newburyport Harbor anymore.

She sat up, startled. The *Maximum Liquidity* was under way.

She thought back to the charts she had seen on the dining room table.

The North Atlantic.

She was sailing the North Atlantic.

And somebody was going to be very surprised when he, or she, or they, for that matter, found out that she was on board.

Chapter 3

EDDIE'S MOTHER HAD PAID for the repairs to the *Maximum Liquidity* after its accident off the Newfoundland coast. She had also paid for its upkeep—marina fees, maintenance, and supplies—at least until Eddie lost all her money. Of course, the boat had a lot of emotional resonance for Helen as well—after all, her husband had lost his life on board.

For his part, Eddie barely had the resources, from his bartending job at Maddie's, to pay for his own life, let alone the boat. As a result, *Maximum Liquidity* was anything but. It could have been renamed the Negative Cashflow, because the boat was racking up debts at the Newburyport Harbor marina that nobody in the Noonan family had the resources to deal with. As a result, Eddie didn't feel comfortable approaching the marina in daylight, either to take the *Maximum Liquidity* out for a spin or even just to go on board and make sure that the boat was truly seaworthy. All of his preparations, therefore, including the buying of maps and the laying on of provisions, took place under cover of darkness, after the harbor master and others who worked at the marina had all gone home. Somehow, he had never crossed paths with Kathy.

Eddie waited for the first moonless night in order to steer the *Maximum Liquidity* out of its slip. He did so by catching a ride from Marblehead to Newburyport with one of the other bartenders, who gave Eddie a ride in exchange for his coveted Thursday, Friday, and Saturday night shifts at the bar. She dropped him off half a block from the harbor, just after three in the morning, without a soul in sight.

Eddie took advantage of the darkness and rushed quietly to the dock where the *Maximum Liquidity* floated peacefully. He was startled by a sound behind him. Scanning the darkness for movement, his eyes finally settled on the black lab. It sat about five feet away from him, eagerly vying for his attention.

"Shoo, Guinness!" Eddie whispered through the dark. "Get lost!"

The dog began whining and moved around in place. It edged closer to Eddie as he began untying the boat. Just as Eddie pushed off, Guinness jumped aboard.

"Great," thought Eddie, "Now what do I do? Throw you overboard or tie back up?" Eddie considered the dog for a moment. Neither of them had homes to return to, and the ocean was a very lonely place. He could use some company. Besides, feeding Guinness would be easy, he'd been living off of table scraps for years.

With that, they headed for open waters. Luckily, the tank was still full of gas. If it hadn't been, Eddie would have had no means to refill it.

You could say he had left everything behind, but everything didn't amount to much—a failed investment company that had taken his father decades to build, his own reputation in tatters, little in the way of material goods, and no meaningful personal relationships.

As Eddie set sail and slowly began his journey, the wind was calm, with the New England coast, hours from sunrise, only occasionally dotted with light, he felt two things: a sense of freedom, and a feeling that he had never been so alone in his life.

In terms of accuracy, one out of two wasn't bad.

The only sounds were gentle waves lapping against the hull of the yacht as it slowly plowed north on the first leg of its journey to Ireland and the occasional crackle of the marine radio. The Coast Guard was engaged in the business of rescuing two extremely drunken sailors from a vessel that had run out of fuel somewhere in the vicinity.

It might have been a moonless night, but it certainly wasn't a starless one. The further Eddie sailed from civilization in the form of eastern Massachusetts, the more stars shone brightly and coldly in the predawn dark sky. It made him think about the one family vacation the Noonans had ever taken on their boat, a trip to Bermuda interrupted when a precipitous market selloff drew Ned to the mainland and back to work. The darkness, the quiet, and the awareness of water rushing softly past the boat reminded Eddie, oddly, of the first minute or so of the Pirates of the Caribbean ride at Disney World, where he had taken his girlfriend on a weekend jaunt, just because neither of them had ever been there. How far away that whole life seemed now.

Suddenly Eddie heard some thumps from below decks. Guinness ran after the sound and began barking intently.

His first thought was that the ship had rats, but that made no sense. Newburyport Harbor was not known for being rat-infested.

Eddie tensed. Suddenly it dawned on him that he might be alone on the high seas with some crazed homeless person. He had heard that individuals were sleeping in boats, but he had never believed that anybody might have been sleeping in his boat. It seemed too unbelievable. Eddie was terrified—what if a lunatic really was down there? Somebody who had already lost everything and therefore had nothing left to lose? What would happen next? Was the guy armed? Dangerous? Well, who wouldn't be dangerous, armed or unarmed, if he were cornered in a small space like a boat in the middle of the Atlantic, as this guy clearly was? Eddie nervously looked around for a suitable weapon, but he couldn't find anything more threatening than a serrated steak knife from the galley. The boat never went far enough to warrant a need for a weapon for self-defense.

The *Maximum Liquidity* cut quietly through the pre-dawn waves as Eddie, who could feel his heart pounding in his chest, crouched in the shadows by the steep stairway that led below decks, waiting for whomever was down there to make his move.

In the captain's cabin, the intruder had gone silent as well. Kathy had heard the unmistakable sounds of a human being above and reacted with the same terror as Eddie. Guinness' barking made her particularly nervous. She wore a T-shirt that she had slept in, and little else. She looked around the darkened cabin, lit only by the faintest glow of dawn making its way through the portholes, seeking out something she could use as a weapon to protect herself from whatever violence, or unwanted advances, her unexpected host might have in mind.

As was the case for Eddie, nothing presented itself as a true weapon, except for the baseball bat she had carried with her since the night she had slept in the Volvo in the alley off Comm Ave.

The standoff ensued for several long minutes—Eddie, silent, crouched above decks, armed with nothing more than a decent, if worn, steak knife, and Kathy down below, her hands gripped tightly around the base of the bat, her heart racing as well.

"I've got a gun," Eddie suddenly heard himself say, surprising himself with the statement, which was untrue, of course. "Come up now or I'll come down and shoot you."

To his immense surprise, and even relief, a woman's voice responded.

"Don't shoot!" he heard Kathy exclaim. "I'm not dangerous!"

Slowly, Eddie crept down the steps while at the same time Kathy, not releasing her tight grip on her baseball bat, made her way out of the shadows of the captain's cabin toward the same steps. It was still so dark that neither could see each other, and they both moved so stealthily that neither could hear each other until they were six feet apart.

Suddenly Eddie and Kathy saw one another for the first time, dropped their weapons, and screamed. Guinness followed suit, barking at Kathy next to Eddie's side.

"You scared the hell out of me," Eddie said, as he realized that Kathy was completely unthreatening, and not bad looking, either.

"You scared the hell out of me," Kathy replied, breathless, as she quickly realized that Eddie had no gun and that his only weapon, the steak knife, had clattered down the stairs past where she was standing. He returned to the top of the stairs and allowed his guest to come topside.

"Sorry about the thing with the gun," he said sheepishly. "I just had no idea who was down there."

"I'm sorry I've been crashing on your boat," Kathy said. "This is your boat, right? Or are you doing the same thing I am?"

Eddie shook his head, as he gave Kathy an appraising look. Not bad for a stowaway, he thought. "It's my boat, all right."

"It's a nice one," Kathy said.

Eddie nodded, as he headed for the coffee machine, glancing at the instruments on the control panel. All was well.

"It used to be my dad's, but that's a story for another time."

"I haven't got anything but time," Kathy said. "By the way, where are we going?"

Eddie blinked a couple of times as he started to make the coffee. "Ireland," he said. "At least that was my plan."

"Ireland?" Kathy repeated, stunned. "I thought you were gonna say something like, you know, Martha's Vineyard. Or Nantucket. But Ireland?"

"We're already a long way from Martha's Vineyard and Nantucket," Eddie said. "That's the Maine coast over there, and we'll get to Nova Scotia by this afternoon, and then we're across the Atlantic. Unless you have a better plan."

Kathy thought about her situation for a long while.

"Ireland sounds really good right now," she admitted. "Anyway,

I hope you don't mind having a first mate."

"Do you have any sailing experience?" Eddie asked, as the coffee hissed into life.

"The only experience I've had on a boat," Kathy admitted, "is breaking into yours."

Eddie sighed. "I guess that'll have to do," he said, his vision of a solo journey vanishing. He didn't want to turn around and go back to the States. It was entirely possible that if he tried to do so, his boat would be impounded for having failed to pay the marina fees back at Newburyport. And his guest might have been a stowaway, but she didn't appear to be dangerous.

"I didn't catch your name," Eddie said, setting down a cup of coffee on the galley table where Kathy had seated herself.

"Kathy Drucker," she said, and she extended her hand to Eddie.

"Edward Noonan, Jr.," Eddie said, shaking her hand and sitting opposite her. "But everybody calls me Eddie."

"Do I have to call you Captain?" Kathy said, sipping her coffee, which was perfect.

"I wouldn't mind it if you saluted once in a while," Eddie said.

Kathy shrugged and smiled. "I guess, under the circumstances, I can manage that," she said, snapping off a salute. "Did you say we were going to Ireland?"

"Roger that," Eddie said, studying Kathy. "Now, who on earth are you, and what are you doing on my boat?"

Chapter 4

DAWN BROKE, SKIES WERE clear, and in the distance, the Maine coast could be seen, seven miles to port. The route Eddie had plotted would take him along the coast, up to Nova Scotia and Newfoundland, and then across to Ireland. The benefit was that he would stay within sight of land for the maximum amount of time possible before heading out into the open seas of the North Atlantic.

Eddie and his unexpected guest, crew member, or stowaway, depending on how you wanted to look at it, sat silently as the sun rose, contemplating this unexpected turn in their lives.

Kathy spoke first.

"It really is a nice boat," she said admiringly. "I'm guessing that you're very rich."

Eddie gave a pained expression. "Used to be," he admitted. "This boat's about all I've got left."

Kathy, puzzled, studied him.

"I don't think I've ever heard that one before," she said. "'I'm down to my last yacht.'"

"I pretty much lost everything else," Eddie admitted. "I know it sounds kind of crazy. The boat was the only thing in my name."

"And what about this guy?" Kathy asked, looking at Guinness, who was now happily panting by her side.

"Guinness and I kind of found each other. He doesn't really belong to me. We're just pals," Eddie responded, looking at the dog fondly.

"And what wasn't in your name?" Kathy asked.

"Everything else," he said. "My condo, my cars, my company. Actually, it was my father's company for 33 years, and it was mine for a year and a half. That's all I needed to wipe it out. Oh. And my model girlfriend. It turns out she wasn't in my name, either."

"Bummer," Kathy said agreeably. "Must be tough to lose all that."

"They say it builds character," Eddie replied, "but I say character is overrated."

"You really had all that stuff?" Kathy asked. "A company, a condo, cars—"

"Don't forget the money and the model girlfriend," Eddie said. "Not that I can forget them."

"And you really only have a boat left over?" Kathy asked, studying him. "You must have a couple of million in an account somewhere, right?"

Eddie laughed. "The lawyers and forensic accountants found everything," he said. "Including a couple of accounts with a couple of million dollars in it."

"The ones you saved for a rainy day?" Kathy asked, teasing him.

"Exactly," Eddie said, grinning ruefully. "Apparently we had too many personal assets in the corporate name so the judge decided to let them take everything." "I'm still not sure why they didn't take the boat. I guess I got lucky."

Kathy shrugged. "So what's your plan? Live on the boat?"

Eddie shook his head. "Can't afford to," he said. "Haven't got a dime. I had to steal my own boat out of the marina. I was so far behind in slip fees, it's incredible they didn't padlock the thing."

"I didn't know they padlocked boats," Kathy said, rubbing her chin. "That's interesting."

"Not if it's your boat," Eddie countered. "There's nothing interesting about that at all."

"So what's your plan?"

Eddie shook his head. "I could tell you more about what happened, but the bottom line is that I'm basically unemployable in Boston. Or anywhere in America, in finance. I'm pretty good at bartending, but that's about as far as it goes for me."

"I'm a pretty good waitress for a lawyer," Kathy said. "I think I can identify. Not with the millions, or the girlfriend, or the condo, or the cars for that matter. But at least the part about not exactly living up to my full potential."

"And what is your full potential?" Eddie asked playfully.

"It's hard to say now," Kathy said. "I think I'll be too busy spending the rest of my life paying off my law school loans even to figure out what my potential is supposed to be."

"That's bad," Eddie said.

"You could say that," Kathy agreed.

Eddie checked the gauges on the boat's control panel and saw that everything was going fine. The waters were calm, the wind was up, and they were making decent time. Not that Eddie was in any particular hurry, now that he was on the high seas.

"So why were you living in my boat?" Eddie asked. "Did you say you were a law student?"

Kathy shrugged. "Used to be. And I had a great and glorious future ahead of me with Sykes & Martland. Until they wrote me a letter telling me they wouldn't be needing my services as an attorney, but they would be thrilled to have me back as a paralegal."

"Ouch," Eddie said. "My firm used to run their money."

"Well, they certainly didn't have any left over to pay me," Kathy said, with a tinge not so much of bitterness but of disappointment in her voice.

"We kind of lost just about all of their money," Eddie admitted sheepishly.

"Some of that was probably going to be my salary," Kathy said. "Well, I guess I never really wanted to be a lawyer anyway."

"What's plan B?" Eddie asked.

Kathy gestured around the boat. "You're looking at it," she admitted. "I got a job waitressing in Newburyport. But it wasn't paying the bills after I racked up all that debt from taking out my student loans. You know how that goes. Or maybe you don't."

Eddie nodded. "I didn't, but I learned," he said.

"So…" Kathy started, thinking out loud, "What you're trying to tell me is, despite the opulence of your watercraft, if I may use that term, you're actually a member of the nouveau poor."

Eddie thought for a moment. "I don't particularly like the sound of that," he said. "But I think it's all too accurate. Nouveau poor it is. And you?"

Kathy shook her head. "We've always been poor," she said. "This is nothing new for me. Although crashing in somebody's boat? I guess that is a new low."

"Why were you doing it?" Eddie asked. "And…what's that line from Casablanca? Out of all the boats in Newburyport Harbor, what made you walk into mine?"

"I like quality," Kathy said, and they both laughed.

"Can I ask you a question?" Kathy asked.

"You've asked me about a hundred so far," Eddie said. "What's one more?"

"Are we really going to Ireland?"

Eddie hesitated. "Eh, I'm starting to second-think the trip, given this new development of a stowaway on board. I should probably head back to land."

"What? No! There's nothing for me back there. You and I are better off at sea."

Eddie thought for a moment. Even if he did go back, returning to the marina was no longer an option. They may let him in, but based on the amount of money he owed them for slip fees and maintenance, they certainly wouldn't let him back out. Besides, there was a weather system forming behind them that Eddie would prefer not to deal with. He thought about making a beeline for the coast but realized he couldn't exactly tie up, have Kathy step off the boat, and leave her off the coast of Maine. He quickly realized that if he changed course now, it would certainly bring about a whole new set of potentially undesired variables. The most logical solution would be to continue on.

"Wouldn't anyone be looking for you?"

"Nope," she answered. "Anybody who would want to is probably upset with me or after me for rent."

"Don't you have family that would be worried about you?"

"Since you told me your story, I may as well tell you mine. My mother died when I was a teenager. She was the closest person in the world to me. She was diagnosed with cancer and put up an amazing four-year battle. In the end it metastasized and spread through her entire body. I was at her side from the first day of her diagnosis to her last breath. I had to be; my father completely fell apart. He got depressed and withdrew himself emotionally. I don't know the textbook definition for a mental breakdown, but I'm pretty sure he had one and never recovered. The doctors had him on so many antidepressants, I barely knew who he was after a few weeks."

"What about your brothers and sisters?" said Eddie.

"Sometimes it's not so great being an only child," she replied.

"You, too?" said Eddie."

"Yes...Anyway, he was remarried within six months of her death, and as you could probably imagine, I didn't have a relationship with his new wife. We've practically been strangers ever since. I set sail—so to speak—on my own after my mom's death and have been taking care of myself ever since."

"I'm very sorry to hear that." Eddie felt a pang of sadness for her. He thought about losing his father.

"I'm past the pity and sympathy. Things are fine now. Anyway, all that is to say that there isn't anything waiting for me back there. I want to hear more about why you're headed to Ireland."

"The short answer is what I told you," Eddie said. "I'm unemployable in my field anywhere in the United States, and probably anywhere on the planet. I'm pretty good at bartending, and I heard they have a lot of bars in Ireland."

Kathy shook her head. "They have a lot of bars everywhere," she said, quietly but firmly. "Don't you think you have an obligation to explain to your stowaway exactly why she's going to Ireland and not some other place?"

Eddie bit his lip. This was a little more than he wanted to reveal, but he figured, what's the difference.

"My father was going to Ireland on this boat," he said. "But there was a storm, and he didn't survive. I was supposed to go with him, but I bailed. I feel like I kind of owe it to his memory to complete the trip."

Kathy pondered the information.

"Wow," she said.

Eddie said nothing.

"Is that how you ended up taking over your father's company?" she asked.

Eddie nodded.

"And it was so successful that it ran money for law firms like Sykes & Martland?"

Eddie nodded again.

"And you made such a mess of things that you drove it out of existence in eighteen months, and that's why you're running away to Ireland?"

Eddie sighed. "I think you summed it up pretty well," he said, slapping his thighs. "Everything I told you is exactly right. No company, no condo, no money."

"No model girlfriend," Kathy interrupted, completing his sentence. "You don't have to remind me. She split when the money was gone?"

"That would make her sound like a gold-digger," Eddie said, pretending to be indignant. "She actually waited a week, to see if it was coming back. It wasn't, and that's when she hit the trail."

Kathy took in the information. "Hey, what does a girl have to do to get some breakfast? What kind of cruise is this, anyway? Where's the menu? Where do I order my meals?"

"I'm not much of a cook," Eddie admitted.

"Well, as it happens, I am," Kathy replied. "Are you a good tipper?"

"Used to be," Eddie said. "It's tough to tip when you can't afford to eat out."

"Amen to that," Kathy replied. "I'll cook if you do the dishes. I hate doing dishes."

"I think we can work something out here," Eddie said. "I'd love to hear more of your story, but I'm pretty exhausted. I didn't get any sleep last night. I had to steal my own boat out of the harbor, and then I found I wasn't alone. It's been a traumatic day."

"Poor baby," Kathy said. "It sounds like you need a nap."

"And two eggs, over easy, and hold the sarcasm," Eddie said, giving her a teasing look.

"Aye, aye, sir," Kathy said, snapping off a mock salute and heading for the galley.

"Why don't you just make your own breakfast," Eddie suggested. "I'll eat when I wake up."

"Breakfast for one coming up," Kathy said. "Roger that, Captain."

"I like that," Eddie said, nodding thoughtfully. "You call me Captain, and I'll call you…"

"Tennille?" Kathy said. "You know, like the Captain and Tennille?"

Eddie rolled his eyes. "Just my luck," he said. "A stowaway who thinks she's Jay Leno."

"I always saw myself more as the Letterman type," Kathy said. "Have a nice nap."

Eddie was about to give her a smart answer when he thought the better of it. A stowaway, he thought. Unbelievable. At least she can cook.

He headed down to his cabin to grab a nap.

Chapter 5

EDDIE COULDN'T SLEEP.

This isn't what I wanted, he told himself, over and over again, as he tossed and turned. He thought of Kathy sleeping in the Captain's Cabin.

The whole point of this trip was to go alone, he reminded himself. It was nice to have company, but if he had really wanted company, he could have found some at Maddie's back in Marblehead on any night of the week. In a lot of ways, Kathy's presence defeated the whole purpose of the trip, which was to have some time for aloneness, quiet, and introspection. Maybe try to figure out a better way to live his life. It was fun to banter with her, that was true. But Eddie knew that he had never heard of anybody bantering his way to a better life.

And a better life is what Eddie really wanted. It wasn't about money, although Eddie had no idea how much he would miss it, now that it was gone. Okay, he missed the power that money conferred, but he found that he didn't really need all the toys, prestigious condo, even a hot girlfriend. So it wasn't about the money; it wasn't about the feeling of walking down the street knowing that you ran an incredibly successful investment firm, especially when the success of the investment firm had been none of your doing and you were only responsible for its undoing.

The boat was great, although Eddie knew that as soon as he got to Ireland, he would sell it, since he held clear title to it and the marina back in Newburyport was unlikely to be able to enforce a lien against him in Galway Bay or wherever he ended up.

Or maybe he would keep the boat and live on it, as Kathy had suggested. Why not? He wasn't likely to find accommodations anywhere this nice in Ireland. Although he wouldn't be fitting into a community if he were living on his boat. But maybe fitting in wasn't the most important thing.

No, Eddie decided. It was. For the first time in his life, he was going to find a community and enter it on his terms—not as his father's son, not as heir to a family fortune, not as a legacy at some yacht clubs. For the first time in his life, his first name, and not his last name, would make the difference.

And the trip across the ocean was intended as a means of honoring the memory of his father, and as an opportunity to think things through. Eddie didn't understand how he would be able to think anything through as long as he had company.

On the other hand, Eddie thought, she was kind of fun. Her life was pretty much in the same unhappy situation as his, but she was maintaining a good attitude about the hand fate had dealt her. She wasn't a complainer. He liked that. She seemed to be taking her reversal with a lot more equanimity than he had faced his.

And she could cook.

Maybe it could work, he reasoned, shifting his weight on the bed. Maybe it wouldn't be the worst thing in the world to have a little company. If the seas got rough, always a possibility in the North Atlantic in the springtime, it wouldn't hurt to have another pair of hands.

I guess I have to make the best of a bad bargain, he told himself. But maybe it wasn't that bad a bargain. If he had to have a stowaway, at least it was someone whom he could talk to. And if they stayed awake in shifts, which made the most sense, once he taught her the basics of steering and overseeing the boat's autopilot system, he would still have plenty of time to himself to think. As long as the food holds out. He really hadn't planned on provisions for two.

Maybe we can catch some fish, Eddie decided. It was the last thought he had as he dozed off.

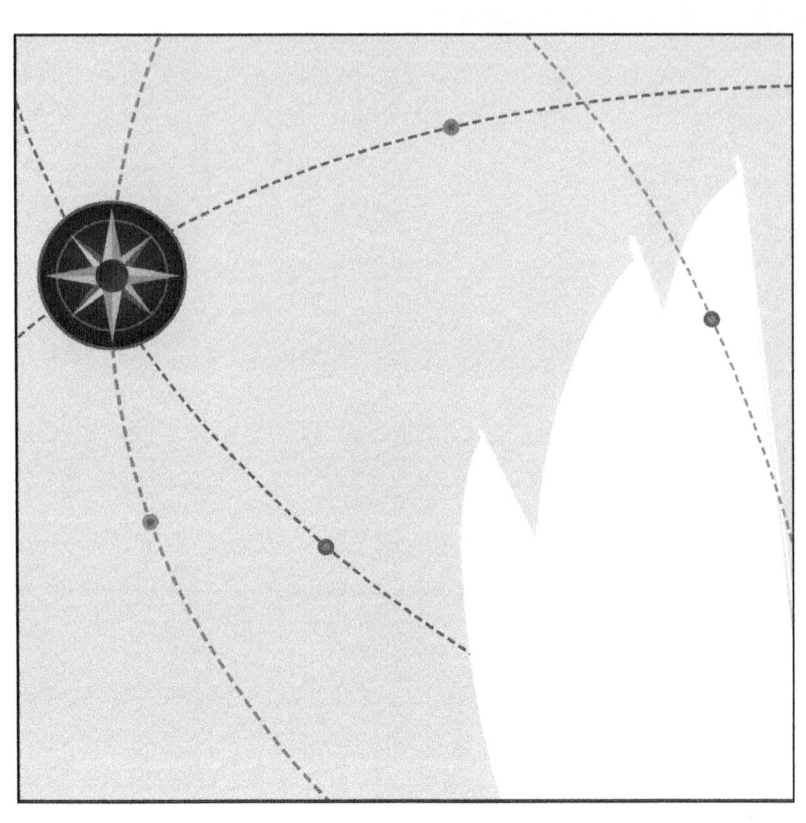

Chapter 6

IT DIDN'T ADD UP, Kathy thought, as she went to work in the galley to make herself some eggs. His whole story seemed preposterous. How could a guy own a boat this big…and nothing else? She glanced up at the sails and wondered how exactly the boat stayed on course. She knew nothing about boats, or sailing, or the kind of people who owned boats. Certainly, some of the partners at Sykes & Martland owned boats, because she saw pictures of them in their offices and would often hear them talk, on summer Monday mornings, about weekend trips they had taken to Nantucket or Martha's Vineyard, places she had heard about but had never seen. It seemed amazing to her that someone as young as Eddie could own a yacht this big. She had heard of wealthy people roughly her age, but she couldn't remember ever having met one. He couldn't have been out of his early thirties, and the partners at her firm, the ones who owned boats, all looked like they were in their late fifties, no matter how old they really were.

She took one more glance up at the sails, which were billowing in the light breeze, allowing the boat to cut through the slight chop that the ocean presented, wondering how exactly the whole autopilot thing worked. It must have worked fine, because otherwise Eddie would never have gone downstairs for a nap. She opened the refrigerator and found eggs, butter, and other recently purchased groceries that Eddie must have brought on board with him the night before. Certainly the refrigerator had never been so full in all the time that she had spent as a uninvited guest on the boat. She scrutinized the galley, which she had glanced at but never really examined thoroughly in her time on board. It was really perfect, a gourmet kitchen in miniature. Everything you needed was right at your fingertips, she realized, as she quietly opened the drawers and peeked inside. Everything—the knives, the pots and pans—those of the highest quality. Whoever Eddie was, he sure knew how to live.

Or did he, she wondered, as she cracked the eggs and began to scramble her breakfast. If his story was even half true, if he had lost his job and all his worldly possessions, except somehow for the boat, what did that say about his knowledge of life? Not very much. Kathy assumed that people like Eddie, people who grew up rich, were given more than just a great big pile of cash when they turned eighteen or twenty-one or whatever.

In addition, they also got all the keys to a successful life, whatever those keys were. Connections to other wealthy people, who would always be there to give you a job. Knowledge about what to do with money—how to invest it, how to deploy it, how to make sure you never ran out. In her limited experience with wealthy people, Kathy realized, she had never met one who had gone from having a lot of money to a condition much near her own—not having any. Until now.

Certainly, the partners at Sykes & Martland must have been going through some belt-tightening if they had to eliminate her position and, presumably, so many others. Kathy was certain that she wasn't the only one who got fired. But people like the partners at Sykes & Martland gave the impression of having buckets of cash stored away for a rainy day. She had no doubt that even though the firm might not have been making as much money for them, they had plenty left. Eddie, as far as she was concerned, was in a category all his own.

And why Ireland? Was Eddie Irish? Did he know anything about Ireland? Had he ever been? Or was that a lie, too? Who would just pack up and leave everything behind and sail solo to Ireland? What kind of person did something like that, she wondered. Successful people took vacations, but they didn't just up and leave. They stayed put, year after year, decade after decade, just like the partners at Sykes & Martland, making lots of money, and doing with that money whatever wealthy people do. Eddie seemed like a good guy, but either he was a liar who had concocted this whole crazy story about losing everything, or he was a fool, if the story was true. In the meantime, she was, she realized, at his mercy. He didn't seem like the type who would do anything violent or dangerous, but out here, in the middle of nowhere, you never knew.

Kathy thought for a few moments and studied the steak knives. Hadn't there been one in Eddie's hand when he was coming down the stairs to check her out?

What was good for the goose was good for the gander, she thought, and then she wondered where that expression came from, and wasn't the goose male and the gander female? No matter. She studied the steak knives, glanced down the stairs toward where Eddie was presumably sleeping, and selected from the top drawer a small steak knife that came with its own protective sheath beneath it. She pocketed the knife and went back to making her breakfast. Better safe than sorry, she decided. Eddie didn't really seem the type to do something bad, but the circumstances were unusual, and you never knew.

You never knew.

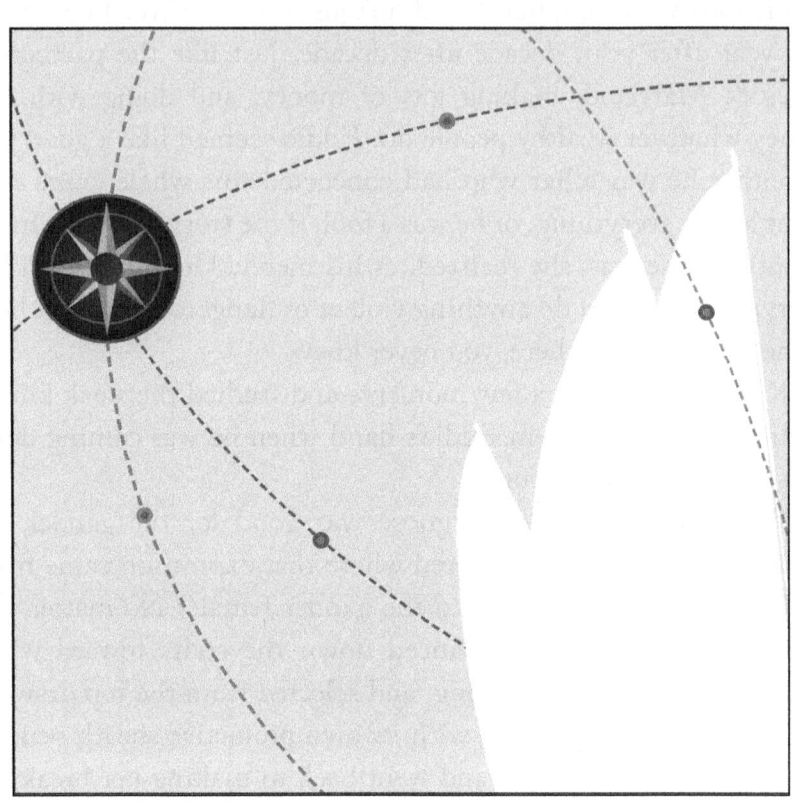

Chapter 7

THAT AFTERNOON, EDDIE awoke with the dry mouth feeling of not knowing where he was or for how long he had slept. Instead of a twenty-minute nap, Eddie had actually taken an eight-hour excursion into REM sleep. His fatigue had been brought on by a combination of two factors: one, the gentle rocking of the boat as it neatly sliced the waves of the North Atlantic off what was now the Nova Scotia coast; and the exhaustion resulting from staying up all night to cut the boat loose from its slip without being caught.

For a moment, he had no idea where he was; the last dream he could remember before awakening was of sleeping on a waterbed that one of his college suitemates had owned. But the waterbed had been more than a dozen years ago. And this was now.

Slowly, his current situation came into focus.

He was on the *Maximum Liquidity*.

He was going to Ireland to start over, or at least to hit the pause button on his life so he could retool it.

And there was a girl onboard.

He sighed and shook his head.

We have to talk, he told himself. Kathy and I have to have a conversation.

He cleaned up and went above decks, where Kathy was stretched out on the deck, enjoying the sunshine, reading a book Eddie didn't recognize.

As soon as she saw him, she sat up.

"We have to talk," they both said simultaneously, and then they both stopped.

"This isn't something I planned," they both said simultaneously, and they stopped again.

Now they looked at each other, each with the expression that said, "You go first."

After a long pause, they both said simultaneously, "You go first."

Then they both laughed.

"This is a really good book," Kathy said. "I'm really enjoying it."

Eddie nodded and looked blankly at her. "Great," he said, having no idea what she was talking about. He didn't recognize the book she was reading, which was more like a spiral-bound document than a book, and frankly, talking about books was really not what he had in mind at that moment.

"We just need some ground rules," Eddie said. "If we're going to make this work."

Kathy nodded. "My thoughts exactly," she said.

Eddie went over to the helm and studied the instrument readouts. He turned and checked the sails, which were properly set for the conditions. He then checked the wind, which was calm, and the water, which was equally calm. He assured that the instrument readings were normal for the conditions and glanced over at the sail trim. His practiced sailor's eye recognized that all was well, and he turned back to the matter at hand.

"It's nothing personal," he began, "but this was supposed to be a solo voyage. I needed time to think things through. My life didn't exactly turn out the way I expected."

Kathy nodded. "I could say the same thing about my life," she admitted. "Everybody said I was crazy to go to law school, that I would hate it and that I would hate the East Coast. Well, everybody was wrong. I liked law school, I like the East Coast, I liked everything except not getting a chance to prove myself. And not having enough money to pay my bills. That's not how we're raised in the Midwest."

"That's not how we're raised in Boston, either," Eddie said. "So I empathize with your situation. But again, I just never really expected to have somebody else on board."

"I never expected to be going to Ireland," Kathy countered. "I think the last few hours have been full of surprises for both of us."

Eddie thought for a moment before he spoke. "Fair enough," he said. "We just have to figure out how to make this work," he said. "Any ideas?"

"I'm easy," Kathy said. And then she looked chagrined. "I don't mean that I'm easy in the sense of being…easy. I just mean I'm agreeable. Whatever we work out is fine with me."

Eddie nodded. "Um, you can take the captain's cabin," he said. "You've kind of made yourself comfortable in there already."

Kathy reddened.

"Believe me," she assured him. "It was never my intention to be sleeping on somebody else's boat. It's just how things worked out."

Eddie nodded. "I understand," he said. "I'll take the other bedroom. I think we ought to sleep in shifts, just because that'll give us each the most privacy, and the most rest. And it's not the worst thing to have somebody awake and at the tiller."

"I agree," Kathy said earnestly. "By the way, what's a tiller?"

Eddie started to point to the tiller, a lever attached to a post that provides leverage for the helmsman to turn the rudder. And then he stopped. "I can give you a short course in sailing," he said, "but it's pretty straightforward on this boat. As long as the waters are calm, the computer pretty much does everything. And then if we get a storm, which is always possible, you just wake me up if I'm sleeping and I'll handle it."

"My hero!" Kathy declared, in mock admiration.

"Well, very funny," Eddie replied, rolling his eyes. "I'm just saying that if something happens—"

"Believe me," Kathy said earnestly, "if something happens, you're not going to be getting any eight-hour naps."

Eddie nodded. "We just want to stay safe," he said. "On top of that, the whole point of this trip was for me to have some time by myself so I could just think."

"I could help you think," Kathy said. "We could talk about some of the stuff in this book."

"This is going to sound embarrassing," Eddie said, "but I'm really not that much of a book guy. I don't even know if I've read a book since Wharton." He shrugged. "Maybe if I'd read a few more books on prudent financial management, I would never have gotten myself into the mess I did."

"Water under the bridge," Kathy said. "Or, more accurately, water under the *Maximum Liquidity*. You've got to be able to just let go of past mistakes. Things happen. You can't keep beating yourself up."

Eddie studied her.

"What are you talking about?" he asked, surprised. "Do you have any idea how much money I lost? How much trust I destroyed? How I took down a business that had taken my father decades to build?"

"Feeling guilty isn't going to get any of that money back," Kathy said. "How do you think I feel, having chosen to come out of law school at the exact time when the entire legal community was in free fall? You don't think I beat myself up for that, do you?"

"I don't know why you should," Eddie said. "You had no choice in the matter. Things just happened to you. This is something I did to myself."

"Either way," Kathy said, "you have to take each day as it comes. The past is the past, and there's no use in dwelling on something you can't change."

"You have a remarkably positive attitude, considering where your life is," Eddie said.

Now Kathy shrugged. "I could beat myself up, or I could just deal with it. Truly, this is not the way I expected my life would turn out. On one hand, my life isn't over. It's just kind of...a glitch. But on the other hand, here I am out on this beautiful boat. Sailing to Ireland. You could make a case that that's a lot better than filing documents for a real estate transaction, sitting in an office, staring into a computer screen."

Eddie thought for a moment. "I see your point," he said. "That's why I love sailing so much."

"I'm just glad I don't get seasick," Kathy said. "That would be bad."

"It's been pretty calm so far," Eddie agreed. "Once we head into open waters, it's going to get a little rougher."

"Really?" Kathy asked, not liking the sound of it.

"What do you expect?" Eddie asked. "It's the Mid-Atlantic in springtime! Didn't your travel agent tell you before you bought your ticket?"

Kathy laughed.

"I'll deal with it," she said. "'Never borrow trouble from the future.' That's what it says in your book."

"I don't know what book you're talking about," Eddie said.

"Don't be so modest," Kathy said. "You still want eggs? I know it's three in the afternoon, but I make a mean Spanish omelet."

Eddie thought for a moment and nodded. "I could live with that," he said. "Maybe having a stowaway on a solo voyage isn't the worst thing in the world."

"Now you're talking," Kathy said happily. She took the book back to the cabin, and she headed to the galley to make Eddie's breakfast, however late in the day it was.

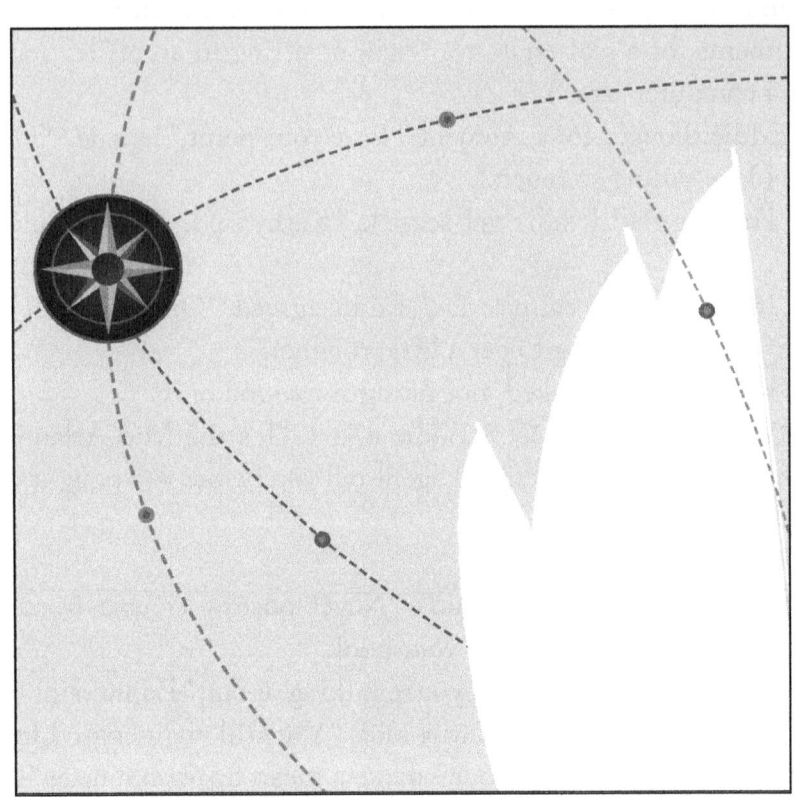

Chapter 8

THE OMELET WAS AMAZING. Eddie didn't realize how ravenously hungry he was until he tasted the first bite. She even made some for Guinness, who ate his portion just as voraciously. It suddenly dawned on him that he hadn't eaten in almost twenty-four hours, his last meal having taken place around 5 at Maddie's, fish and chips, courtesy of the bartender who was going to take over his highly desirable weekend shifts. At that moment, you could have put just about anything in front of Eddie and he would have eaten it up. But he was a veteran of far too many top Boston restaurants, back when he was busy wearing out his American Express black card, not to recognize the extraordinary quality of Kathy's work.

For her part, Kathy watched in silence as Eddie scarfed down the omelet.

"Where did you learn to cook like this?" Eddie asked through a mouthful of eggs.

Kathy shrugged. "Around," she said. "Growing up. Nowhere special."

"It's one thing," Eddie said, greedily polishing off the last of the omelet, "to cook this well if you've got a full-on kitchen. But to whip this up in that tiny little ship's galley? That's incredible."

"Does this mean you're not going to throw me over to the sharks if we get low on food?"

Eddie grinned. "Only if you get out of line," he said. "Seriously, this is the best omelet I ever ate."

Kathy nodded thanks, but Eddie could tell that something was bothering her.

"What's wrong?" he asked quickly. "Do I have some celery stuck between my teeth? What?"

Kathy shook her head. That wasn't it. But there was definitely something.

"What?" Eddie repeated.

"I don't know how to say this without insulting you," Kathy began, choosing her words carefully. "I mean, you kind of have me at a disadvantage out here."

"Really," Eddie said, his tone reassuring, and at that same moment, he noticed what looked like the possibility of darkening skies in the direction they were headed. "You can say anything. We're equals out here."

"Are we?" Kathy asked.

"Well, let's just say that neither of us found our way out here on a winning streak," Eddie said, pondering the cloud pattern. Maybe it was a storm, maybe it wasn't. But it was something that bore watching. The vessel was equipped with a fax that received regular reports from a weather service. The fax worked fine but the weather service operated on a subscription basis. If you didn't pay, you didn't get weather updates. Of course, the subscription of the *Maximum Liquidity* had lapsed long ago. Eddie gave the fax machine a rueful look. He should have had somebody at the bar where he worked renew the subscription with a credit card, since he no longer had credit cards in his own name. He sighed and reminded himself that you can't think of everything.

"Our balance sheets are pretty similar, too, from what you say.

Not a lot of cash on hand, a fair amount of debt, and no real way to repay it. Not a lot of market for hard-earned skills. Although in your case, I think you might have worked harder to get your skills than I did. I just kind of fell into everything, and then fell out again."

"It's true that I've got the boat," Eddie continued, "but if something happened to it, I couldn't afford to repair it. I can't even afford to dock it somewhere. So we have a lot more in common than people might have suspected."

Kathy considered Eddie's words, but she didn't look convinced.

"What is it?" Eddie finally said, a small amount of impatience revealing itself in his tone.

"It's the book," Kathy said simply.

"The book?" Eddie asked, not understanding. "I told you, I'm not much of a reader."

"I'm not talking about what you read. I'm talking about your book."

Now Eddie looked bewildered.

"Let me lay my cards on the table," Kathy said, looking Eddie in the eye. "I just don't understand how somebody could write a book like the book you wrote and have a life that's as upside down as yours."

Eddie wiped his mouth with a cloth napkin and stared at Kathy.

"I really have no idea what you're talking about."

"Your book," Kathy said. Now it was her turn to be confused. "You, Edward Noonan, wrote a book and dedicated it to your son. You never told me you had a son. Not that it's any of my business. But it's the kind of thing somebody would mention, at some point, in a situation like this, or at least that's what I would think."

Eddie's eyes widened. "Edward Noonan?" he repeated. "I'm Edward Noonan, Jr. Edward Noonan is my father."

Kathy's jaw went slack. "Your father wrote that book?" she asked. "I thought you were Edward Noonan."

"I'm Edward Noonan, Jr.," he said. "But everybody calls me

Eddie. My father was Edward Noonan, Sr. Everybody called him Ned. And I don't have a son."

Suddenly Eddie got it.

"Wait a minute," he said, a new intensity in his voice. "My father wrote a book?"

"Didn't you know?" Kathy asked, flabbergasted. "I found it in the back of one of the drawers in the cabin. It was wrapped in plastic, probably to keep it from getting wet or something. I just read the whole thing, I couldn't put it down."

"My father wrote a book and never told me?" Eddie asked. "This is unbelievable!"

"How could you not have known?"

Eddie shrugged. "My father passed away," he said quietly. "I thought I mentioned that. And he never said anything about a book."

Kathy blinked a couple of times. "So you've never read the book," she said, trying to put the pieces together. Eddie shook his head.

"If you've never read it," Kathy said, "then I guess that takes away the whole mystery of—well, okay. I guess I understand. If you had written the book, you probably wouldn't be in the mess you're in. Now if I had read the book a couple of years ago, before I went to law school, maybe I wouldn't be in the mess I'm in."

"It's that good a book?" Eddie asked, amazed that his father had written a book, that his father had written a book without telling him, and that his father had written a book that was so good. Eddie had never known his father to be much of a reader, either, unless it was a stack of annual reports and SEC filings.

"It's that good," Kathy said quietly. "It's one of the most powerful books I've ever read."

"Why didn't he tell me?" Eddie asked, stunned.

"I don't know."

The line of gray clouds definitely meant trouble. Eddie found himself regretting even more deeply the fact that he didn't have that weather service sending him faxes. If he did, he would have had some idea of what they were sailing into.

"Where is it? Where's the book?"

"It's downstairs," Kathy said. "Do you want me to get it?"

"Yes," Eddie said. "Would you mind getting it right now?"

"Sure," Kathy said, astonished by the turn of events. She got up from the table. "I'll be right back."

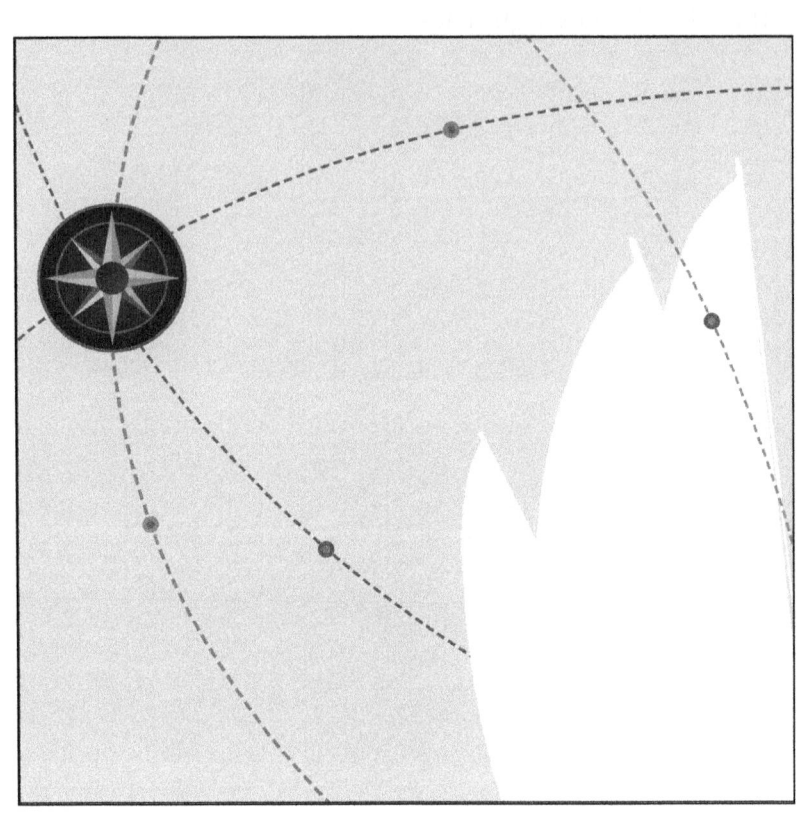

Chapter 9

HIS FATHER'S BOOK WAS called *Adjust Your Sails*. Eddie opened it and began to read...

Chapter One
INTELLIGENT LIFE DESIGN

Ever since I arrived on the shores of this fine country, it has been my privilege to be surrounded by people with money. Some of them were individuals from my hometown who paid for my travel from Ireland and enabled my education. Others gave me my start in my business. As a result of living among, working for, and serving wealthy people, I became one myself! And in my decades of service in the financial community, I have witnessed one phenomenon repeating itself with alarming regularity. So many people put so much effort into their portfolio design, but they completely neglect the design of their lives.

I know this is true, because I have been one of them, and it is my greatest regret.

Prudent asset management requires diversification, and a constant, regular rebalancing of the elements within a portfolio. The larger our position in a particular asset class, the greater our exposure to the vicissitudes of the market in that particular sector. For example, if a portfolio is too heavily weighted toward technology stocks, a tech bubble, such as the one that occurred in the late '90s, in this nation can have a destructive effect on a portfolio. Look at real estate in the late 2000s and you'll see the phenomenon repeat itself. There must be some exposure to risk, of course, because without risk, there is little chance of reward. But the greatest risk of all is imbalance, because overexposure in one area can more than wipe out the hard work and gains that may have taken decades to produce.

There's not a man or woman on Wall Street who would disagree with this premise. An unbalanced portfolio is an invitation to disaster. And yet, while we financial professionals, if we are wise, constantly review our portfolios to make sure that balance exists, so many of us, myself included, have failed to do this in our personal lives. We have failed to put the same exacting care into our marriages and families that we put into our financial portfolios. The result is predictable: imbalance, which spells disaster, at home just as much as it does on the trading floor.

When I say that we financial types live unbalanced lives, I refer to the fact that most of us work extremely long hours, longer still since the introduction of after-hours' trading. The market never truly closes, and even while we sleep, market-makers in London, Tokyo, Beijing, and other points on the globe are hard at work seeking advantages for themselves and their clients, often at our expense. At the same time, those of us who manage money for others no longer have the luxury of burying our mistakes in between monthly or even quarterly statements. Instead, our clients can view their portfolios in real time, minute by minute, seeing where we have risen and where we have stumbled. And we are seldom forgiven for the slightest of stumbles—it's all too easy today to move money elsewhere.

As a result, most of the people I know who work in finance live with a constant case of what used to be called nerves and what today is called stress. We work at the mercy of the markets, in constant fear that we will miss a high or a low, fail to get in or get out, or that forces beyond our ability to manage will lay waste to all our hard work. Beating the market has turned into an onerous chore that saps the energy of the financial professional and all too often fails to occur.

In this highly stressful world, technology represents a double-edged sword. It allows us to trade with a blinding speed unimaginable when I began my career. At the same time, it allows individuals, from day traders to the most cautious retirees, to build, maintain, and trade for their own portfolios, without the guidance of people in our field.

This is our struggle—longer hours, declining returns, more stress, and less time for family, friends, and relaxation. The maxim in our industry is to work hard and play hard, but play, hard or otherwise, has all but vanished from our lives. Not just play, but any sort of adequate time with our loved ones. We struggle to keep our financial portfolios in balance, but in our personal lives, balance is all but a myth.

Obviously this state of affairs cannot last. Or at least our pursuit of happiness is deeply endangered by the way we live our lives today.

The purpose of this book is to help others apply the concepts of balance I've learned through running portfolios to their own life. In asset management, reputations are made or broken as a result of the choices made with regard to allocating assets. In life, the most valuable commodity is time. And yet, few of us apply nearly the same level of conscious thought to the allocation of our time as we do to our more tangible assets. If we were to apply portfolio theory to time, we might live very differently.

We would recognize how unbalanced our lives often are. We would recognize that we can win a million dollars in the lottery, or we can earn a million dollars with a particularly shrewd investment. Yet we can neither win nor earn a million hours. We can, perhaps, add years to our lives through healthy living and the avoidance of certain bad habits. But there is no website or Bloomberg device that will allow us to see just how much of our most precious commodity, time, we have left.

Navigating through life is not too different from keeping a boat on top of the water. Life often brings its own currents and wind in the form of challenges and problems. It took me a long time to realize that you can't fight the current. Instead we must navigate through our own existence guiding the boat with what we have. The sailor must ultimately work within the framework that is set forth by nature. In life, your mind is the rudder and your heart is the sail. Your heart measures the energy and captures its essence to guide you forward in the general direction you desire. Your mind is the tool used to fine tune that direction and serves as the operations center. When you allow the two to work in lockstep without one overpowering the other, you begin to realize that you do have an amazing amount of control over your life's direction.

These sorts of musings may seem odd coming from an individual as notoriously "left-brained" as myself. But these are the things we must consider if we are to avoid the all-too-common situation in which we find ourselves—making a living but failing to make a life.

So humor an old fellow for a little while and consider this concept—if you apply the concepts of balance utilized in portfolio construction, to your life, you begin to realize that time, not money, is the most precious asset that we possess. Just as we apply intelligent design to our financial portfolios, we can apply the same concept of intelligent design to our lives.

I speak not necessarily with the greatest of wisdom, but I do speak with considerable experience. I hope that my experience, positive and negative, will offer you valuable guidance, so that you can avoid the mistakes I made. And let me say at the outset that I am not necessarily the greatest of role models. I have led an unbalanced life, devoting far too much of my time to my work life and not nearly enough to my wife and son. Perhaps some will see this book as my effort to make amends to them. Many of you reading these words may be experiencing similar challenges in your own life. If you are, ask yourself, "What steps can I take today to begin to bring each of these relationships back into alignment?" Stop reading and fill in the chart below. Seriously. Stop reading.

Taking just a few minutes to think about your life and how you can honestly change the direction of it.

Takeaway #1: A balanced life is just as valuable as—if not more valuable than—a balanced portfolio.

Takeaway #2: Consider your mind the rudder and your heart the sail to your own vessel. You have amazing control over the direction of your life.

Takeaway #3: Your time—not your money—is the most valuable asset that you possess.

Action Step 1:

List three [3] things in your life that are out of balance:
1. _____
2. _____
3. _____

Why are these things out of balance?
1. _____
2. _____
3. _____

What specifically can you do to help bring your life into balance?

Item 1:
    Change 1: _____
    Change 2: _____
    Change 3: _____

Item 2:
    Change 1: _____
    Change 2: _____
    Change 3: _____

Item 3:
    Change 1: _____
    Change 2: _____
    Change 3: _____

When will you begin to integrate these changes into your life? Add the required action steps to your calendar, daily to-do list, or whatever system you use to ensure that you get the desired results for the items you listed.

※ ※ ※

"Whoa," Eddie said, eyes widening. He felt the skin on his neck and shoulders tingling. It felt as though his father was speaking to him—he didn't want to think. He just wanted to keep reading. Guinness had fallen asleep next to him and was beginning to snore quietly.

At that moment, however, the storm that had caught his eye a few minutes earlier looked like it might be gathering strength. He gave a thought to calling out to Kathy, but instead he stretched out his back and settled back into his father's book.

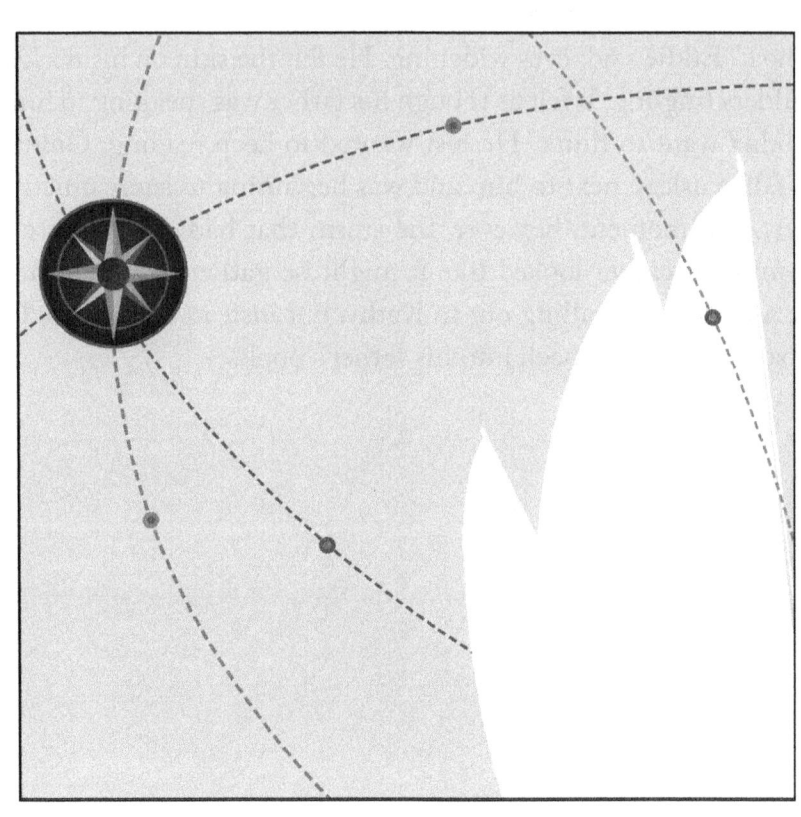

Chapter 10

MINUTES LATER, KATHY APPEARED on the stairs and gave Eddie a concerned look.

"Is it my imagination," she said, as Eddie looked up from the ship's controls, "or did the waves get a little…bumpier?"

Eddie's face relaxed into a grin. "I'm not quite sure that bumpier is a nautical term," he told her, "but yes, it's a little choppy out there."

"Shouldn't we, you know, find land?" Kathy asked nervously. "Is it safe?"

Eddie's expression was reassuring. "I've been in a lot worse than this," he told her. "It's just a little chop. It's really no big deal. You'll see. The storm will pass, and as far as I can tell, it's actually not going to pass anywhere near us."

"Then why is the 'little chop' so…choppy?" Kathy asked. "To use the proper nautical term."

Eddie shrugged. "That's just how it is," he said. "We'll pass by a storm, but we're not going through it. And that can make for slightly rougher seas. But it's no big deal, and we don't need to look for land."

Kathy paused for a minute. "Okay," she said dubiously. "I've just never been out on a boat like this before. It's all new to me."

"We'll be fine," Eddie said.

"Did you read any of your father's book?" Kathy asked.

Eddie nodded ruefully. "He was talking to me," he said.

"Not just you," Kathy replied, taking a seat opposite him. "He could have been talking to just about anybody. He certainly could have been talking to me."

"He was speaking directly to me," Eddie said.

Kathy nodded. "What was that like," she asked carefully, "reading your father's words like that?"

Eddie shook his head. "It's hard to find words to express exactly what it felt like," he admitted. "I never even knew my dad wrote a book, let alone that he had anything he wanted to tell me." He paused. "Actually, to be honest, I tuned him out years ago."

Kathy studied Eddie. "How far did you get?" she asked.

"Just the first chapter," Eddie said. "Why?"

"Then you saw the part about him apologizing for not having more of a balanced life," Kathy said. "It's not your fault."

Eddie shook his head firmly. "That's just Dad being Dad," he said, chagrined. "My dad led the most balanced life you could imagine. Work, family, exercise, church, friends, and this boat. If my dad was saying anything like that to me, he was taking responsibility for something that was clearly my fault. I thought I knew everything and I didn't need any help from him. It turns out that I didn't know very much. I took his money and I took the jobs he gave me, but I never really tried to learn from him."

Eddie paused.

"I guess that's why he wrote this book. To say to me the things that, well, he always wished he had said. No. To say the things that he probably always wished I would have listened to."

"There's nothing worse than a trust fund baby who's run out of money," Kathy said, lightening the mood.

Eddie extended his right hand in the air, as if he were in a courthouse, being sworn in.

"Guilty as charged, Your Honor," he said. "It is kind of pathetic, isn't it?"

"I don't think so," Kathy said earnestly. "Everybody goes through lessons. Yours just had more dollar signs on it."

"It was an expensive lesson, indeed," Eddie said soberly. "You can't imagine what it's like."

"You might have been down to your last boat," Kathy reminded him, "but I'm the one who was sleeping in it."

Eddie reddened. "Point taken," he said. "But the thing is, it wasn't your fault. You couldn't have foreseen that the market for lawyers was going to crash."

"I suppose," Kathy replied. She grinned. "I have a high school friend who used to say, 'Hindsight is 20/20.' You look back and you see the amount of billable hours we racked up as a result of the real estate bubble, deals that should never have been done that we were profiting on. You had to realize that couldn't go on forever."

Now Eddie grinned. "You didn't need it to go on forever," he said. "Just for another twenty years."

Kathy tossed her hair. "Same thing," she said. "It's no big deal. Now I'll just have to figure out how to make an honest living."

"Most lawyers are honest," Eddie said. "At least the ones we dealt with at Forecastle."

"They may be honest personally," Kathy said. "But their whole business model is flawed. It was driven by an unsustainable bubble. That's what couldn't last. I should have seen that coming. There are plenty of other ways to make a living as a lawyer. And you get to serve society, too."

"That's what always happens when people lose big money jobs," Eddie said, teasing her. "They try to figure out how they can serve society."

Kathy gave him a dirty look. "Cheap shot," she said. "I don't know exactly what your profession does for society."

"Hey," Eddie said, putting up both hands in mock defense. "Just remember, good money managers help their clients to educate their children and retire comfortably. They sort of protect their investors from themselves. Left to their own accord, most people would get fearful and sell low, then turn around and buy high when the greed of missing out on an opportunity kicks in. Unfortunately, I can no longer include myself in that group of good money managers. Hell, I don't even have a profession anymore," he reminded her. "Except maybe bartender."

"You could always get a job driving boats," Kathy said.

"Sailing boats," Eddie gently corrected her.

"Whatever," Kathy said. "So what else did you get out of Chapter One?"

Eddie held the boat steady. The waters were definitely getting choppier.

Eddie thought for a long time before he answered. "I liked what Dad said about applying portfolio theory to life," he said. "I've never thought of that. We spend so much time designing portfolios for our clients, making sure that there's no imbalance. Correcting when necessary."

"I hope you're a better sailor than you were a money manager," Kathy said, teasing him.

"Cheap shot," Eddie replied, pretending to look hurt. "I guess I had that one coming."

Kathy smiled. He did.

"It's amazing how people—okay, not people, how I let my life drift. I just figured I'd be running Forecastle forever, I'd have all that money forever. I just figured I was set. Turns out there is no such thing."

Kathy nodded thoughtfully. "I bet that's what a lot of the lawyers at Sykes & Martland thought," she said. "They thought they were set, too."

"I guess there's no such thing," Eddie agreed. "I never saw it that way before, though."

Eddie kept a hand on the steering wheel and stared out at the sea.

"So what are you going to do differently?" Kathy asked. "I mean, did the book make that much of an impression on you, that you'd do things differently?"

Eddie shrugged. "I don't know how I can do things differently," he admitted. "I don't have anything to do. I'm totally unemployable in my profession. In my former profession," he added, correcting himself. "Who would hire the guy who turned The Forecastle Group into The Foreclosure Group?"

"I would," Kathy said.

Eddie stared at her.

"For what?" he asked. "I've got no skills, other than losing a lot of money and mixing a mean Long Island iced tea. And you don't exactly have a job to offer me, do you?"

"You could work at my new public interest law firm," Kathy said, teasing him. "You could be the bartender at our fundraising events."

Eddie rolled his eyes. "I do want to do things differently," he admitted. "I'm ashamed of what I did to my father's company. I'm ashamed of what I did to my life. I'm ashamed, period."

"That's a start," Kathy said, shifting her weight on her chair and eyeing the waves uncomfortably. "Are you sure this storm isn't coming anywhere near us?"

Eddie checked his instruments again. "It'll come a little closer than I thought. We might get a little rain. But nothing serious."

"That's good, I guess," Kathy said doubtfully. "Wait 'til you read what your father says about shame in Chapter 2."

Eddie looked at her in surprise.

"Dad talks about shame in Chapter 2?" he asked, surprised. "What does he say about it?"

Kathy gave him a wide grin.

"You're going to have to find out for yourself," she said. "I'm going downstairs to straighten up. The place looks like somebody's been living in it."

"Ha ha ha," Eddie said. He watched her go, and then he turned his attention back to steering the boat.

Chapter 11

EDDIE KEPT AN INCREASINGLY concerned eye on the weather as he went back to the table where he had left his father's manuscript. He retrieved it, sat back into the worn creases of the leather helm and flipped to chapter two. It was the most bizarre feeling for him—the sensation that his father was reaching out to him, from a distant place, to provide the guidance that Eddie might not have been able to hear, understand, or appreciate while Ned was still alive. On top of that, Eddie was increasingly conscious of the fact that the boat was approaching the place where his father had lost control of the *Maximum Liquidity* in a late spring storm, and that another storm, but most likely not of the same intensity, was brewing now.

Chapter Two
WHAT'S ON YOUR SCREEN?

One of the greatest days in the history of my career was the installation of our first Quotron unit in our offices at Forecastle. Today, that Quotron would look like a museum piece to young, technologically attuned financial people, but at the time, it was a Godsend. Thanks to the Quotron, we could quickly ascertain the current value of the shares of any company trading on the Big Board, the New York Stock Exchange. In our industry, which is so dependent on current information, it was an absolute game-changing experience to have the Quotron handy at all times.

Technology evolved, of course, and before long, no self-respecting financial firm could afford to be without its Bloomberg devices, screens which provided in real time a wealth of information that enabled us to make wiser decisions, in the blink of an eye, if necessary.

Technology for the home evolved as well, to the point where practically all of us find ourselves surrounded by screens from morning 'til night. At the office, we have sophisticated computer equipment lining the trading floor. At home, big screen TVs resembling nothing less than concepts from a Buck Rogers' serial of my youth, grace our family rooms, bedrooms, and even "home entertainment centers."

And along with those massive screens we enjoy an equally massive selection of channels—the satellite package to which we subscribe in our home provides at least a thousand channels of entertainment and sports, but only if you can figure out which of the three remotes actually makes the TV work!

So the question at work and home is no longer, do you have a screen or two or five for your viewing pleasure, because pretty much all of us have that. The real question is this: What are you watching? Just as television or the Internet provide a seemingly endless array of options, so does life. In my den, I have the power of choice (at least when I'm alone!). I can watch a football game from halfway around the country or a soccer match from halfway around the world. I can watch shows about cooking and I can watch shows about killing. The choice is mine. Whatever I turn my attention to crowds out all other options. Yes, there is some sort of split-screen apparatus that the installer demonstrated for me, but I must admit I never got the hang of it. I'm old-fashioned. I can only watch one thing at a time.

I find those big screen TVs and Bloomberg units at work to be an apt metaphor for the way life really is. We have endless choices, but we can pretty much only choose one viewing option at a time, whether it is sports or drama or cooking or whatever. In life, I can only be in one primary relationship at a time. I can only devote my energy to one particular portfolio or trade at a time. I can devote my thoughts, however fleeting they may be, to one concept or idea or memory or plan at a time. Anything I pay attention to, obviously, grows in importance in my mind. There may be 999 other channels, other ideas, other people, other deals, other relationships, but right now I have my mind focused solely on one.

If I have a well-trained mind, I can maintain my focus for long stretches of time. If my mind is unruly, it may jump from subject to subject, but for each of those moments, however brief, I was focused on one particular thing. This reminds me of the Buddhist concept that the mind consists of a chariot and horses. We and our minds are two separate entities—we are either the chariot or the horses. We direct our thinking—we lead our mind—to where we desire it to go. If our mind is the horses, it drags us, the chariot, willy-nilly, across some path or no path. In other words, if we aren't careful, our minds can be the ultimate off-road vehicle!

So if I have been granted the power of focus, it stands to reason that the more effort I put into developing focus in life, the happier and more successful I will be. So I must choose carefully what I focus my attention on, which of the thousand channels I tune to. Yes, those other 999 channels are waiting for me, but they are not where I have chosen to place my attention. As a result, it is as if, in that moment, they do not exist for me.

Again, so it is in life. Whatever I pay attention to takes on the energy that I put into it, as if it were a television program that I have selected or a stock I am watching on my Bloomberg at the office. Every program on television creates a different sense of energy within me. Sports gets me excited. Cooking shows lull me to sleep. Travel shows excite me with the possibility of the plan of a new trip. And so on. We are all affected differently, in accordance with our own tastes. But the universal truth is that I'm not just tuning into a program. I'm tuning into a source of energy, positive or negative, constructive or destructive. This is true whether I am tuning into a program on TV or tuning into a situation or concept in my business or personal life. I am either increasing or decreasing my energy level, based on the choice that I have made.

If it's so obvious when we sit on our couch with all those remote control devices in front of us, why don't we see the same reality when we apply this concept to our lives?

Physicists tell us that little is as solid as it seems. The table upon which my Bloomberg device at work rests looks as solid as anything in the universe. It is a beautiful piece of carved mahogany. And yet, as solid as it may appear to me, and as heavy as it is when it needs to be moved, it is nothing more than a whirling mass of electrons, protons, and neutrons, an energy field that has taken the shape of...a mahogany table in my office with a computer terminal balanced upon it.

Our lives seem, in many ways, as solid and unmovable as that mahogany table. But nothing could be further from the truth. Just as that table is a whirling mass of electrons, so are we! So are the choices we make. We are energy. Our energy is enhanced or diminished by the choices we make, but we are constantly in flux, just like the uncountable trillions of cells that make up our physical bodies.

Eddie paused for a second and shook his head in wonder. *Dad knew all this?* he thought, amazed. He continued to read, with renewed admiration for his father, an increased sense of wistfulness that he had never known this aspect of his father's philosophy of life.

Energy in, energy out. That is how our lives go. Everything is energy. Love is energy. Money is energy. Reputation is energy. And emotions are energy. Indeed, our emotions are the gateway to energy in our lives, because the choices we make trigger emotions within us, and those emotions in turn trigger an increase or decrease in the quality of the energy with which we live our lives.

A simple example. How do you feel going to work the night after you've had a fight with your wife or husband? Not that great, right? And then it seems as though everything else goes wrong. Your car won't start. Traffic is worse than usual, or you missed your train. At work, your computer fails to function! Your hunches about the direction of the market prove inaccurate, and irate clients, watching their portfolios dip in real time, call you to demand to know the reasons why.

All because you had a fight with your wife?

Conversely, your team has made it to the World Series, and through connections with a client, you and your best friend have seats right behind home plate. Your favorite pitcher throws the game of his life, and your team has won the World Series for the first time in countless years. You were swept up in the celebration, get to bed on three hours' sleep, float into the office not even remembering that you actually drove your car there, and every trade you make turns magical.

All because your team won the World Series?

Perhaps. Actually, the word "perhaps" is inappropriate. All these things happened, negative or positive, because you attracted them. In the first case, your energy was dragged down by the disagreeable evening with your spouse. In the second case, your energy spiked because of the adrenaline rush of watching your team win big. Energy is a magnet. It draws like unto like.

This is the explanation of streaks, in sports, in our personal lives, and at work. When our energy is random, we get random results. When our energy is negative, we draw to ourselves negative results. When our energy is positive, well, I don't need to state the obvious. Energy is a magnetic force. We tune into a particular brand of energy, positive or negative, and the result is what we would expect—not unlike making a choice about what we're going to watch on our big screen at home or what stock we're following on our computer screen at the office.

To return to the metaphor of the horses and chariot, we have our emotions and we have our intellect. Either our emotions will drag our intellect around willy-nilly, randomly, and all too often destructively, or we will make the decision to have our intellect direct our emotions. I call this putting the capital letter I, for Intellect, over the E, for Emotions. There are times when negative emotions are appropriate. When we lose, we must mourn. When we win, we must celebrate. But too many of us live as captives of our emotions, and thus find ourselves dragged down to a negative emotional state too much of the time, which leads to low energy, which leads to bad results.

It is as if there were, in addition to the Discovery Channel and the History Channel on our widescreen TVs, a Depression Channel. It doesn't show footage of the Great Depression of the 1930s. Instead, it is a constant, unending, unavailing repetition of negative emotions that leads to a sense of depression in us. And yet all too often, our viewing habits would indicate that we watch the Depression Channel to the exclusion of everything else that is available to us! No wonder our energy is not what it could or should be. No wonder our results are not what they could or should be.

So I pose this challenge to you. How should your energy be? Negative or positive? Attracting success, love, fun, and happiness, or repelling them? We have all made mistakes, and yet some of us remain trapped in a constant replay of those mistakes in our minds. We are tuned to the Shame Channel, and we show ourselves internal home movies of the mistakes we made, in an endless loop. This is not—not— an appropriate use of the God-given mental apparatus we all enjoy.

My purpose in writing this book is to challenge you to determine what sort of energy you create for yourself. Is it negative or positive? If it's negative and you blame others for the results you unconsciously create with that negative energy, to put it simply, is that any way to live?

Or do you place the I over the E, your intellect over your emotions, such that you choose what energy you tune into, just as you choose what channel to watch at home?

I'm not suggesting that there's a Euphoria Channel that you can tune into 24 hours a day. I am saying that we humans could do a much better job of running our lives, but only if we make the conscious decision to put that I over the E, to allow our intellect to direct our emotions, and to demonstrate to ourselves and the world that we have tuned into, and therefore attract from others, positive energy, powerful energy, life-affirming energy, the energy that drives success at home and at work.

In the next chapter, I'll show you how.

Takeaway #1: Energy is a magnetic force. When our energy is negative, we attract negative results. When our energy is positive, we attract positive results.

Takeaway #2: Energy in, energy out. For every action, there is a reaction. Our emotions dictate the energy in our lives. The choices we make trigger emotions within us. Those emotions increase or decrease the quality of our life.

Takeaway #3: We can only focus our attention on one thing at a time. Focus influences your emotions and creates a starting point for directing your energy. Choose your focus wisely.

Action Step 2:

List the shows you have watched over the past 24 hours. If you prefer, list the shows you will watch over the next 24 hours.

1. _____
2. _____
3. _____
4. _____
5. _____

For each of these shows, state how you felt watching them and whether the show provoked positive or negative emotions:

Show 1: _____
Show 2 _____
Show 3: _____
Show 4: _____
Show 5: _____

After watching the shows with negative emotional reactions, how did it impact any part of your day?
_____
_____

After watching the shows with positive emotional reactions, how did it impact the remainder of your day?
_____
_____

Recognize the connection between the shows you watch and the energy those shows produce in you. Begin to consider other influences in your life. Just as you can change the channel, you have the ability to control your exposure to many external influences.

Think about people in your life who are chronic complainers. Do you enjoy their company? How do they make you feel?

Now think about that person you know that always has nice things to say. They seem perpetually happy and always see the glass half full. How do you feel in their presence?

If energy is all that exists, it would appear that there is a force at work in the universe that is beyond anything we can conceive. Call this universal energy or if you prefer God. We exist within this energy. If we can properly tune ourselves (our energy) and resonate with the flow, we have the ability to be, do, or have anything we can imagine.

Action Step 3:

List 3 positive influences in your life:
_____
_____
_____

List 3 negative influences in your life:
_____
_____
_____

These negative influences lower your energy and become barriers to the achievement or realization of your desires. What can you do to increase exposure to the positive influences while mitigating your exposure to the negative influences?

_____
_____
_____
_____
_____
_____

❂ ❂ ❂

Eddie blinked several times as he finished the chapter. He slid a sheet of paper into the manuscript as a bookmark, and exhaled deeply.

"The Shame Channel," he said to himself, barely audibly.

And then he looked up at the sky, which had darkened perceptibly during the time it took him to reach the second chapter of his father's book.

"This is going to be a real storm," Eddie murmured, sobered both by the words he had read and the increasingly overcast skies. He didn't need a weather service to tell him that they were headed into trouble. He looked longingly at the manuscript. He wanted to keep reading, but he knew he couldn't now. He sighed. This storm was going to require his full attention. And then he could get back to his father's advice.

Chapter 12

"DOWNSTAIRS IS CLEAN AS a whistle," Kathy said, as she emerged onto the top deck.

"You don't call it downstairs on a boat," Eddie informed her. He wasn't being malicious; his tone was matter-of-fact. He was thinking about the book. "You say 'below deck.'"

"Aye, aye, sir," Kathy said, snapping off a mock salute. "I'll remember that going forward, sir." She glanced at the skies. "Looks like rain."

Eddie also looked uneasily at the heavens. "I'm afraid you're right," he said. "These storms roll out of nowhere."

"I'm not much for storms on the high seas," Kathy admitted, taking a seat opposite him. "When we went to Disney World? I nearly blacked out when I did Splash Mountain."

"We'll be okay," Eddie said, a hint of uncertainty in his tone. It looked like a much bigger storm than he had envisioned. "I just finished Chapter Two."

"About the TV channels?" Kathy asked. Eddie nodded.

"So here's what I'm wondering," he said. "Did my energy attract you, or did your energy attract me?"

Kathy thought for a moment. "Probably a little bit of both," she said. "I just can't tell if you're paying me a compliment or not."

"The way I feel about myself these days," Eddie admitted, "I don't even know how to answer that."

"You don't have to," Kathy said. "When you think about it, though, the book makes sense. We're both kind of in the same position. In the same boat," she added, with a grin.

Eddie nodded. "We are in the same boat, at that," he agreed.

Around them, the wind was picking up. "How bad a storm is it?" Kathy asked, trying to keep the anxiety she felt out of her voice.

Eddie shrugged. "Big," he said, studying the instruments. "It looks like we're riding into it. The North Atlantic is famous for these sudden squalls."

"I'm famous for not having remembered to pack the Dramamine," Kathy said.

"We'll be okay," Eddie said, seeking to sound reassuring, but he didn't sound especially convinced himself.

"What are you not telling me?" Kathy asked, studying Eddie closely.

Eddie swallowed hard. "This is the same kind of weather," he began, "that my father must have ended up in. When, you know."

Kathy stared at him.

"What are you saying?" she asked. "Isn't there any way to change direction? Get out of the way of this thing?"

Eddie shook his head. "It doesn't work that way. We couldn't possibly outrun it. We'll just have to go through it."

"Is the boat…up to it?" Kathy asked, glancing around uneasily. Suddenly, the *Maximum Liquidity* looked less like a luxury yacht and more like a child's bathroom toy as it bobbed in the increasingly turbulent seas.

"I'm a pretty good sailor," Eddie said, although he didn't sound absolutely convinced of his own merits. "I'm sure we'll be okay."

"Can we talk about something else?" Kathy asked. "This is really scary."

"Sure," Eddie said, never taking his eye off the water in front of him except to glance down at the dials and controls. "What do you want to talk about?"

Kathy thought for a moment.

"Your father's book?" she asked.

Eddie nodded. "What about it?"

"Just the stuff he said about whatever you pay attention to," she said. "I'm just trying to apply that to my own life. Is your father suggesting that I somehow brought this situation on myself? That something in me didn't want to be a lawyer? That I wanted to be a homeless person, living on somebody's boat and just waiting tables? That's the part I didn't understand."

Eddie thought for a long time before he answered, his attention divided between her question and the roiling waves.

"It's not that exactly," Eddie said, as the first drops of rain hit the dodger. "I mean, did I really intend to destroy my father's company? Are you kidding me? I think about that every single day."

"So what's the deal?" Kathy asked. "Why did these things happen to us? It's not like we're bad people."

Eddie shook his head. "We're not bad people," he agreed, eyeing the increasingly large raindrops that were spattering the dodger. "Things happen. It's called life. Maybe you didn't really want to be a lawyer. You might not have wanted to be homeless, but maybe being a lawyer really wasn't what you wanted to do with your life."

"It's raining," Kathy said. "This is bizarre. I've never been on a boat in the rain. Actually, except for Splash Mountain at Disney World, I don't think I've ever been on a boat."

"Don't worry about the storm," Eddie said. "It'll pass. But just tell me what you think."

"What I think," Kathy repeated. She pondered Eddie's question. "I never wanted to be a lawyer," she admitted. "There. I said it. I could never even admit it to myself. I enjoyed law school but deep down I now realize that I never truly wanted to be a lawyer."

Eddie turned and glanced at her.

"So why'd you do it?" he asked. "Why did you go to law school?"

The rain, coming down harder, began to beat a tattoo on the roof of the boat.

Kathy gestured, as if to say, "Who knows?"

"I guess it always sounded good," she said. "There are all these TV shows about lawyers, and in my town growing up, the lawyers' kids always had the nicest cars. Actually, they had cars. They had everything. I just thought, this is a good way to make money."

The waves were picking up and the boat was beginning to bounce slightly out of the water as each wave slapped against the boat's hull.

Eddie glanced at her, as if to say, I'm still listening.

"But I've just never really been motivated by money," Kathy admitted. "I thought if I had it, I'd be really happy. But what I found out was that whole concept just didn't resonate with me. I've never realized this before, but I really hated practicing law. Everybody's so competitive; they keep ridiculous hours and for what? Ninety percent of them hate what they do. Even the partners I worked with may have earned the right to put in less hours but were just as miserable.

"I remember asking myself, back when I was a summer associate last year, the question isn't, are they going to make me a partner? The question is, would I want to be partners with them?"

"What's wrong with them?" Eddie asked. "They always seemed like good guys when I talked to them."

Kathy shrugged. "You never worked for any of them. I'm sure they're not bad people, but they sure are lousy employers. They're not exactly big on what you could call people skills. My first day at work, these two lawyers take me out to lunch. They ask me a couple of questions about what law school I went to, where I'm from, and then they started talking about a case I knew nothing about. And they just ignored me for the rest of the meal. Were they this way when they got here, or did practicing law turn them into these kind of antisocial automatons? They were both single, too. I was like, don't you guys even see me?"

Eddie grinned, keeping the boat as steady as he could as it slapped against the waves.

"I never saw that side of them," Eddie said. "Whenever I had anything to do with them, we were talking about money."

"I guess that's their happy place," Kathy said. "It isn't mine."

"What would you rather do?" Eddie asked her, raising his voice to be heard over the increasing wind.

"I wanted to teach kindergarten," Kathy admitted, half-shouting. "I love little kids."

"So why didn't you do that?" Eddie shouted.

"You know how it is," Kathy said. "I guess I tried to be something I wasn't supposed to be. Maybe that's why I ended up out of a job. Maybe I'll still get to be a kindergarten teacher, if we survive this."

"We'll survive," Eddie shouted, but his tone was not especially certain. "We'll be fine."

"What about you?" Kathy asked. "Did you want to do...whatever you did? At your father's company?"

Eddie stared straight ahead, keeping an eye on the rain, which was now pounding against the dodger. He did not want to admit this to Kathy, because he did not want to alarm her, but all of the signs on the instruments indicated that the storm would be bigger than anything he had ever been through. Earlier when he checked the signal, he had underestimated the magnitude of the storm ahead. Now, he found himself questioning whether the *Maximum Liquidity* would indeed be able to weather it. How bizarre would that be, he thought. To go down in the same kind of storm my father did.

"No," he shouted.

"No what?" Kathy shouted back.

"No, I didn't want to work in my father's business," he explained.

The boat was bucking like a bronco in the rodeo by now, and he and Kathy were both trying to mask the level of fear they felt.

"I hated finance from the time I was a kid. It just bored me. Just staring into a computer and calling people and buying and selling—it didn't feel like I was adding any value to society. It didn't feel like you were making a difference in anybody's lives. I have respect for financial professionals who actually work with people. You're helping people invest, grow their money, whatever. I probably would have been a lot happier if I were a broker."

"So why didn't you do that?" Kathy shouted louder, to be heard over the wind and the rain that was pounding the boat. "Are you sure we're going to be okay?"

Eddie ignored the question. "If your father runs The Forecastle Group," he explained, "it would look a little funny if you're suddenly in the training program at a brokerage house. People would think, if he isn't good enough to work for his father's company, why is he here? I don't think anybody would have hired me."

Kathy nodded. "If you say so," she shouted. "It's a world I know nothing about."

"It's not a bad world," Eddie said. "It's just not what I wanted."

"What did you want?" Kathy shouted.

Eddie shrugged. "I never really thought about it," he shouted back. "What's the point? It's not like I could have done anything else with my life. There was always an expectation that I'd take over the business."

"You took care of it all right," Kathy shouted, grinning despite her mounting fear.

Eddie returned a rueful smile. "You could say that," he admitted. "I guess I had to destroy it before I let it destroy me. Although I feel pretty destroyed after what I did."

"You did what you thought was right at the time," Kathy shouted. "I'm getting really seasick," she admitted. "I think I want to go below deck and lie down."

Eddie nodded. "Probably a good idea," he shouted. "Let me see if I can get us through this storm."

Kathy gave him a weak smile. "That would be nice," she said, and she headed below deck.

Eddie watched her go, and then he turned his attention back to the weather. The storm was clearly worse than he first thought, and for the first time since he had left the harbor, he began to feel real fear.

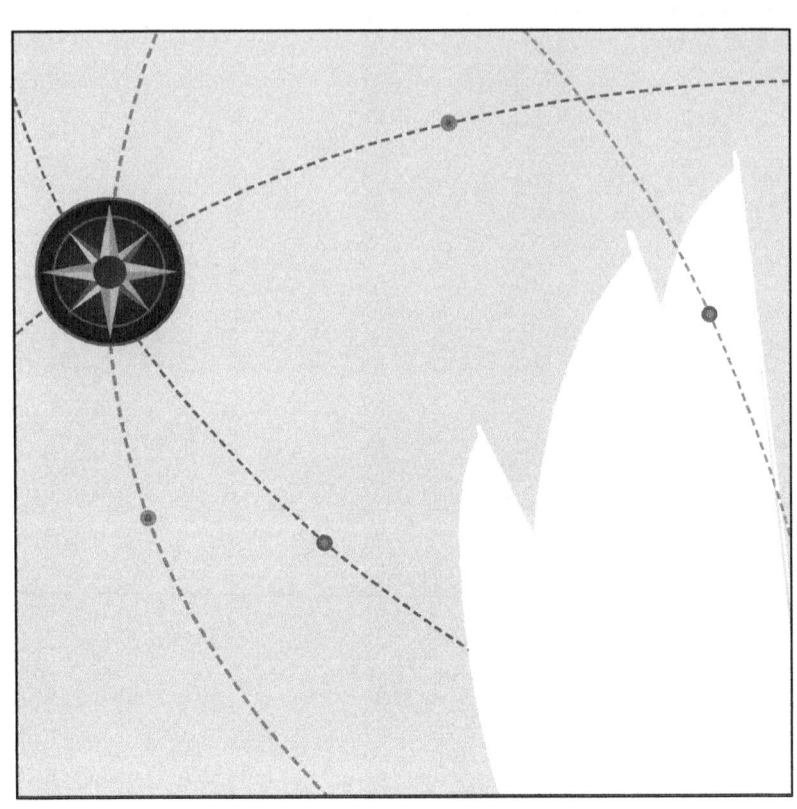

Chapter 13

FIFTEEN MINUTES LATER, EDDIE took a long look at the sky and went back to the manuscript. It seemed to have calmed down for the time being. Guinness sat staring at the clouds in the distance, as if trying to guard the boat from them. Eddie smiled at the sight and dove back into the book. Who knew how long the break in the storm would last?

Chapter Three
ASKING, "WHY?"

By now you may be wondering how to put all these ideas into practice, and I would be remiss if I didn't share an overall philosophy for doing just that. So that's our purpose right now. The purpose of this chapter is to offer an overall philosophy to guide the implementation of these ideas. And it all begins with the key word: Why?

If you have small children, the question most commonly asked in your home is that three-letter word, "why." Children question everything: "Why is the sky blue? Why is there air? Why do I have to eat vegetables? Why do I have to go to bed?" Adults vary in their responses to these vital questions. Sometimes we try to give answers. Sometimes we admit we have no idea why there is air or why the sky is blue. And other times, we simply rely on the verbal equivalent of brute force: "You have to eat these vegetables because I said so." For a child, "I don't know" and "Because I said so" are equally unsatisfying. Indeed, they take the joy out of asking the question "why," and before long, children stop asking it. Instead, their questions focus on the idea of what. As in, "What time can I stay up until? What is there to eat for a snack? What can I do? I am bored."

They're bored not because they don't have enough games to play or enough technology to manipulate. They're really bored because they are no longer asking the most important question in the world: Why?

The human mind was built to ask the question why. We are wonderers by nature. People whose names ring down the ages are those who asked why: Why does the apple fall from the tree? Why does the sun seem to "rise" in the east? Why are we here? And yet, we as parents have entered into a tacit conspiracy to eliminate the word "why" from the vocabularies of our children, even though the greatest scientific, intellectual, and spiritual discoveries have been made by those who dared to ask why. Shamefully, many of us as adults have lost the capacity to ask why about anything important in our lives. So instead, we focus on our own set of what questions: What can I do to make money? What can I buy myself as an unconscious consolation for the fact that my life doesn't possess all the meaning it could?

If you want to implement the ideas in this book, you need to begin with that one critical question: Why? It's the question that so few of us dare even to ask ourselves, but it is the beginning of all knowledge and all experience. Question everything. Question authority. Question yourself. And make the first word of your question the word "why."

When you ask "why," great things happen. Possibilities open up. We shift from a focus of "What do I have to do to succeed?" to a different focus: "Why do we do things this way?" "Why does everybody think this is the best way to proceed?" "Why can't we do it this way instead?" Your why is your starting point, the true north on your compass. Once you start asking "why," you engage the brain at its most fundamental level, as a question-answering machine. "I once had a friend who had a string of bad business deals and he began to ask himself the question, Why do I always fail?" If you ask yourself a question like that, your brain will think and think and think, and think some more, until it comes up with the answer. But if you ask a better question: perhaps one that begins with the thought, "Why can't I…" you engage your brain, the most phenomenal question-answering computer ever created. The simple answer to the question, "Why can't I…" is: "Who says you can't?" No one! Okay, maybe someone. Your boss. Your spouse. The police or the government. Galileo didn't let such matters stand in his way. Neither did Newton. Neither did Descartes, or Tolstoy, or John F. Kennedy. You must always ask "why."

The beautiful thing about asking why, the question we stopped asking as children, is that it reactivates the part of our brain that triggers the how. Most people have an idea or state a desire or intention: "I want to make 10 million dollars." But then they become stymied, because they become convinced that they don't know how to make that happen. If you tell yourself you don't know how to make something happen, you're right. Of course, if you tell yourself that you do know how to make something happen, you're right, too. In fact, whatever you tell yourself, your brain will find a way to make you right. The brain, which drives the ego, hates to be wrong.

So most of us get hung up over the question of how to do something. We assume that since we haven't done something in the past, we never will. Either we won't figure out how or there will be no one to show us how. So the lack of a how keeps us from attaining our goal and ultimately prevents us from making our intention something tangible and real.

What if you came at things from a different perspective? First come at things from a perspective of "why."

Why do you want to have 10 million dollars? What would that create for you? What good would come into your life with that 10 million dollars? Financial security. Confidence that the money is there to take care of all your needs. As a result, you and your spouse will no longer have to fight about bills and money. Your relationship will get better. You will be able to provide opportunities for your children that you might not have enjoyed. You'll be able to live in a nicer neighborhood, drive a nicer car, eat better, join the best gym and hire a personal trainer. And so on.

Of course, some of these outcomes could be achieved without 10 million dollars, but I always say, "If you have a choice between having the money and not having it, have it!" Seriously, I think you see my point. When you think through the why of a matter, why you desire a certain outcome, why you are setting a particular intention, you create something vital: leverage over yourself. The idea of 10 million dollars is simply too abstract for most people, which is why they don't have 10 million dollars. You, on the other hand, are going to create leverage over yourself by listing all the reasons why 10 million dollars is essential to you. Or if not essential, at least highly desirable. Once you create a strong enough why, the how will reveal itself.

Your tools for this are your mind combined with your feelings and emotions, which together form your inner guidance system. Your brain, once it has settled upon the appropriate why, will automatically manufacture the how. And as a result, you will get to the what—in this case, the what being the 10 million dollars.

Again, most people make the mistake of starting—and therefore stopping—with the what. They want the 10 million but they haven't thought through why they want it, and they therefore can't come up with a means of getting it, the how. I say start things from the other direction. Start with the why. Why do I want this? Why do I need this? Why must I have this? Why will my life be better as a result of having striven to attain this? Then your mind will move from why to how. Let it. Your inner guidance system wants to come up with ways to turn your why into a reality, so the why will naturally lead to the how. From there, it's a short step to putting the how into gear, and simply doing the things that your inner guidance system has suggested to you.

Of course, not all of you reading this will be successful in making your why real by doing the "how" steps your brain presents. Why you ask? Lack of discipline or motivation that is potentially covering an underlying fear. Many in the psychological world refer to this as success reluctance. The key is to identify the irrational emotion behind it by starting your own internal dialogue with "why." You will eventually reach the root of the issue. Once there, you are now able to see things from a more rational prospective. This mindset will often remove the roadblocks and allow you to move forward.

So there you have it. How do you turn all of these ideas into reality? What's the starting point? Get leverage on yourself by asking the why questions. Your brain will automatically develop the how, and the people and places you need to turn your dream into reality will automatically come into your life. This is a law of nature, an axiom of the law of attraction. And then the what you seek can be yours.

I know it sounds simple, but when you think about it, failure is simple, too. Failure is focusing on the what and not the why. If you have done that so far, you're not alone. All of us who were children—which means all of us—were told to stop asking why. I'm telling you to start asking that question again. It is the starting point to making your dreams come true.

Remember that in any enterprise, the employee knows how, but the boss knows why. Be the boss of your own dreams. Ask why.

Why not!

Takeaway #1: Although the greatest scientific, intellectual, and spiritual gains have been made by those who dared to ask why, most of us as adults have lost the capacity to ask why about anything important in our lives.

Takeaway #2: When you think through the why of a matter, you create leverage over yourself and enable your brain to begin processing how you can achieve what you want.

Takeaway #3: Human beings are wonderers by nature. Hone this instinctive habit in yourself and stay curious about the world.

Action Step 4:

Identify three [3] things in your life right now that you want, whether it is resolving a relationship problem, a professional goal, or a long-term purchase, and ask yourself why you desire them:

I desire these in the next 30 days:
1. _____
2. _____
3. _____

Why I desire these things 3 things in the next 30 days:
1. _____
2. _____
3. _____

I desire these things in the next one [1] year:
1. _____
2. _____
3. _____

Why I desire these things in the next year:
1. _____
2. _____
3. _____

I desire these things in the next 5 years:
1. _____
2. _____
3. _____

Why I desire these things in the next 5 years:
1. _____
2. _____
3. _____

What actions can you take to move yourself incrementally closer to reaching each goal? Integrate those actions into your daily activity list.

Eddie paused his reading to take another long look at the sky. At some point soon, he would have to stop reading and deal with the storm. A quick glance at the sails and he noticed the mast had a chip in it. After closer inspection, he decided it was minimal and went back to take in one more chapter.

Chapter Four
CLARITY

You now possess the rules by which the game of life is played. You understand that the much discussed law of attraction comes down to a simple fact: You choose the channel your brain tunes into, and you are responsible for the results. Perhaps not everything in life can be explained this way, but most things can. You are the author of your own life, the captain of your own destiny, and the creator of your own problems. If you have problems, you created them for a reason, even if unconsciously. It's because there is some choice you wanted to avoid, some decision you didn't want to make, some aspect of your life you did not want to face up to. You're not alone. But then, in our society, the unhappy outnumber the happy by a shockingly high margin.

So how do you move from the majority, whose lives are marked by drift, simply by being the byproduct of the environment, the victims, to the minority, those who know what they want, seek it out, accept full responsibility for their life situation and experience the joy that comes from a fulfilling life, a life well-designed and well-lived? You move to the phase of the game I call the search for clarity.

Imagine that you have six months left on Earth and you are fully aware that this is so. Your doctor has informed you that the condition is incurable; a second and third opinion, from equally or more trustworthy medical experts have concurred and reinforced the fact that your expiration date is six months from today. What would you like to accomplish in these six months? Are there people with whom you'd like to spend time? Places to visit? Things to do?

Now skip ahead to your funeral. It sounds bleak, but the truly bleak thing is to die without having lived. You're not going to let that happen to you, are you? What is being said about you in your eulogy? What is missing that you wish would be said? Is there something you could do now to make that happen? What would it be?

A movie called "The Bucket List" introduced millions to the concept that we need to make conscious decisions about the things we wish to do while there is still time on the clock, sand in the upper half of the hourglass. Those who do not take the extremely intelligent advice of this film and fail to create their own bucket list are living the fantasy that they will never die, that there will always be time to do the things they wish to do, and that they need not even enumerate their desires, because there will always be time for that as well.

I'm here to say that's nonsense. A life fully lived avoids drift as if it were a medical infirmity. A life fully lived should encompass the development of a list like this, because although we can win a million dollars in the lottery, or earn it, or worse, inherit it, we cannot win, marry into, or inherit an extra million hours of life. You get what you get. What will you do with what you have gotten? How will you maximize the time that you are here?

I learned little from my father, but I do recall the expression for which he was well known in the pubs of his native Ireland: We are not here for a long time, but we are here for a good time. For my father, goodhearted and loving of people as he was, while sober, his bucket list was quite simple: Drink, drink, and be merry.

I wanted a different life, and I knew from early childhood that I would set my intention on attaining a different life, and I have. It was on my list to make something of myself in the world, to build something important and well regarded that would stand the test of time—

Eddie swallowed hard as he read those words. He knew his father was speaking of The Forecastle Group, and he wondered just what his father would be thinking now. He tried to dismiss the thought and kept reading.

—and I would like to believe I have done just that.

I have raised my son more effectively, one might say, than my father raised me. I have developed a reputation for honesty and integrity which, like the business it underlies, will survive my passing. It is no small thing for people to pass one's burial spot and say, "Here lies an honest man."

So if you ask me now what remains on my list, the thing I would like to do the most is to sail on my own boat across the North Atlantic to the Ould Sod, my native Ireland. I cannot explain why this particular journey draws me so, but I only know that it does. I came to this country as a child with nothing but a child's desire to have a better life, confidence in mathematics, and the blessing and goodwill of my village. I have returned to Ireland many times, to see family, to play golf, and to revisit the touchstones of a long ago childhood. But the allure of sailing my own craft, retracing the route of my original journey, which was powered by others, to be powered simply by the wind, the elements, and what knowledge I gained of sailing in my adulthood—this exerts a pull like no other. With the possible exception of the bouncing of grandchildren on my knee, this life could provide me with no greater thrill than a voyage like that.

And then at my funeral they can say, "He arrived thanks to the power of others and he returned on his own power." Or words to that effect. Somehow the great Irish genetic gift of poetry eluded me! But no matter. I'll leave to others to compose the actual words of my eulogy. It is my responsibility to create the contents of that speech, through the life I live. Incidentally, I never understood why they refer to the time we have left as the "rest" of our lives. This is hardly a time to rest. This is the time to be most active, most dedicated, most committed in the pursuit of our desires. Joy, however, comes to those who seek and appreciate it. Be in the company of those who seek joy, because life demands no less.

And again, I can act or I can drift, but there is no middle ground.

So what about you? You may not die in six months' time, and I hope you do not, but you will die one day. Will there be a song in your heart, because you lived your life to the fullest? Or will there be regret, for the things untried, the people unknown, the dreams unfulfilled or perhaps even undreamt?

These are the difficult questions you must ask yourself, but whoever told us that life would be easy? Indeed, life is easier for the dreamer, because the dreamer has a yardstick by which to measure the content of his days. Those who drift have no map, no guide, no markers on the trail, no buoys to indicate the path toward their dreams. What kind of person do you wish to be? Are you creating a life based on intention or chance?

Takeaway #1: You are the author of your own life, and often the originator of your own problems.

Takeaway #2: We will never know how much time we have left. Experience life now. Do the things you want to do. Live the life you want to live today.

Takeaway #3: Joy comes to those who seek it.

Action Step 5:

Imagine you are a witness at your own funeral. What would your friends and family say about you? Write your eulogy from the perspective of those around you.

_____
_____
_____
_____
_____
_____
_____
_____
_____
_____
_____
_____
_____

Save a copy of that eulogy.

Now rewrite your eulogy from the perspective of how you would want it to be.

_____
_____
_____
_____
_____
_____
_____
_____
_____
_____
_____
_____
_____

What was said in the second version that was not in the first? Create a list of those items and set a goal to achieve each one. Begin to take the action steps today to bring each goal incrementally closer to reality.

Action Step 6:

Create your bucket list. But ask your question in a grander way. What would you like to accomplish while you're on this planet?

We all come across things we would love to do. How many of us have compiled a formal list of things to do before we die? Take the opportunity to do it now. Fill in 10 spots for your bucket list. Include a time frame for doing each.

1. _____ Time frame: _____

2. _____ Time frame: _____

3. _____ Time frame: _____

4. _____ Time frame: _____

5. _____ Time frame: _____

6. _____ Time frame: _____

7. _____ Time frame: _____

8. _____ Time frame: _____

9. _____ Time frame: _____

10. _____ Time frame: _____

❁ ❁ ❁

Suddenly, thunder crashed in the sky. Rain instantly followed, as if some unseen force had pushed a lever that quadrupled the intensity of the rain, the wind, and the size of the waves. Water began to cascade over the top of the boat, soaking Eddie as the boat pitched and yawed, slapped sideways over and over again by the tumultuous ocean. When the first wave crashed over the top of the boat, Kathy ran to find Eddie. Guinness began to run in wild circles barking and whimpering at the same time. He finally ran below deck to Eddie's room and shook himself dry. Eddie closed him off so that he wouldn't run back out. Then he started to contemplate what to do next.

"We. Are going. To die!" Kathy shouted, with a very ominous cadence. They were the only words she could utter.

"We're going to be fine," Eddie shouted over the din of the storm, wrestling the tiller but instead finding his arms practically yanked off by its strength. The tiller seemed to have a mind of its own, and there was no hope really for directing the boat; merely for saving it.

"Do something!" Kathy yelled.

"I'm trying!" Eddie said, at the same time finding her shrieks of terror an unwelcome distraction and also feeling intense compassion for Kathy, who certainly hadn't bargained for any of this. He instantly regretted not having turned back to land the moment he'd become aware of her presence.

That's when it hit him: This must have been the same kind of severe storm that had taken his father's life. Eddie resolved that it would not take his, and Kathy's, as well.

The wind was howling, a low perceptible moan that gave both Eddie and Kathy the feeling that there was some sort of living force behind the storm, or a complaining, angry spirit that had been aroused for no reason other than the fact that the boat was trespassing in the territory that belonged to the sea. The wind continued to howl and waves of increasingly greater size slashed repeatedly at the hull of the boat, terrifying Eddie. Suddenly there was a loud crack as intense as a gunshot, and Eddie, at the tiller, and Kathy, still kneeling on the deck, whipped their heads around to see what had happened.

To Eddie's horror, the main mast had snapped, and the sails, soaked beyond usefulness, billowed helplessly over the deck and then, with the coming of the next wave, vanished over the side of the boat altogether.

"Eddie!" Kathy broke him out of his trance.

Kathy's expression was one of total horror, and Eddie's eyes quickly calculated how much longer the boat could survive. Instead of trying to figure out what to do to salvage the situation now, he started to think about his father going through the same thing. Indeed, when the *Maximum Liquidity* had been recovered after the accident that had claimed Ned's life, the mast had been snapped in practically the same position.

Eddie had spent good money—his mother's good money—repairing the boat, and putting in a new carbon-fiber mast that was guaranteed not to break in all but the roughest conditions.

These obviously were the roughest conditions.

The wind continued to howl, the waves breaking over the top of the ship in increasing number, speed, and strength, and Eddie looked helplessly at where the mast had stood, wondering what to do next.

He reached for the microphone to call for help, but it was useless—the antenna for the boat had been tied into the mast. He couldn't possibly broadcast, not that anyone else could possibly help them. For the first time in his life, and despite the presence of Kathy, cowering with fear, he felt absolutely, completely alone.

He realized that the only thing that could possibly save the boat would be to rig a spare set of sails to the broken mast and somehow force the boat out of the circular pattern it had begun to take on.

Suddenly Eddie remembered something his father had once told him—every storm has a beginning, a middle, and an end. There had to be an end to this storm, if only Eddie could point the boat in one direction and steer out of it. It was a desperate measure, because the boat was rocking so mightily that he knew that if he went back to put up the second mast, he could easily be swept overboard in a heartbeat. But he considered his options and realized he had no others.

"Take the tiller!" he shouted at Kathy.

"What?" Kathy asked, unable to hear him in the pounding storm.

"Take the tiller!" Eddie all but screamed. He motioned to her because she still couldn't hear him. Kathy found her feet somehow, rose, and slowly, carefully, picked out a path to the helm.

"Just keep her as straight as you can," Eddie shouted in her ears. "I'm putting up another sail."

Kathy stared at him, unable to speak, and took control of the tiller. It was as hard to control as a rodeo bull, but she held on for dear life, watching Eddie disappear around the deck.

"Where are you going?" she yelled, but Eddie couldn't hear her and wouldn't have answered anyway. There was no time to lose.

Kathy was petrified. She had never been in a storm this bad before. If I ever get out of this, she thought, I am retiring my sea legs. She went between looking ahead of her to see if she could spot any breaks in the clouds in front of them and twisting her head around to search for any sign of Eddie. So far, nothing.

Meanwhile, Eddie rustled through the various items of the ship's gear until he found what he was looking for—a spinnaker pole to jerry-rig a mast. Feverishly, he pulled them out of the supply cabinet.

Eddie, who never got seasick, felt as though he was on the verge of it now, as the boat continued to pitch crazily, battered by every wave that smashed into its side. He closed his eyes for a second, tried to clear his brain, and moved quickly, if unsteadily, back to the tiller where Kathy was.

"I need your help!" he yelled, his voice barely cutting through the wind and rain.

Kathy, struggling with the tiller that would have taken superhuman strength to keep on track given the forces of nature that sought to control it, stared at Eddie and yelled, "What are you doing?"

"You'll see," Eddie shouted back. "Come with me!"

"I can't leave! What if the whole boat flips over?"

"It won't take that long!" Carefully, cautiously, he led her to the aft of the boat, his precious bundle of gear held close to his body. One good wave, he knew, could knock both of them, the backup mast, and the backup sails into the North Atlantic. He shivered because he did not want to die like his father.

Somehow, with the wind and rain all but blinding him, he made his way to the place where the mast had stood.

"Help me with this," he instructed Kathy. Time was of the essence. She helped him remove what remained of the old mast, and he worked fast to install the new piece. They both used all their strength to hoist the sails.

"Come on!" coaxed Kathy. She grabbed Eddie's arm and ran back to the tiller and regained control of the vessel. It continued to rock but not as violently as before. At that moment, the storm became perceptibly less violent—only marginally so, but at least it was something, Eddie thought.

"Go below deck," Eddie shouted. "It's safer down there."

She shook her head. "I'll stay up here," Kathy shouted. "I'm just too scared."

Eddie nodded understanding and took the tiller from her. He looked in front of him to see that the new mast and sails, somehow, were holding. He took a deep breath and jammed the tiller as hard as he could, trying to keep it straight. The boat was still rocking at a 70-degree angle every six to eight seconds as another massive wave crashed into it. Eddie steered toward what light he saw, and there wasn't much, just a distant speck of clarity on a horizon that was otherwise gray or black. He held the course, using every fiber of his strength to keep the boat from capsizing, glancing ahead every few moments at the new mast. It was their only shot. Twenty minutes later, wracked with exhaustion, the muscles in his arms on fire, the storm had begun to abate. It was still raining, but not nearly as heavily. The wind had died down to where it was possible to hear oneself think.

They knew the worst was behind them.

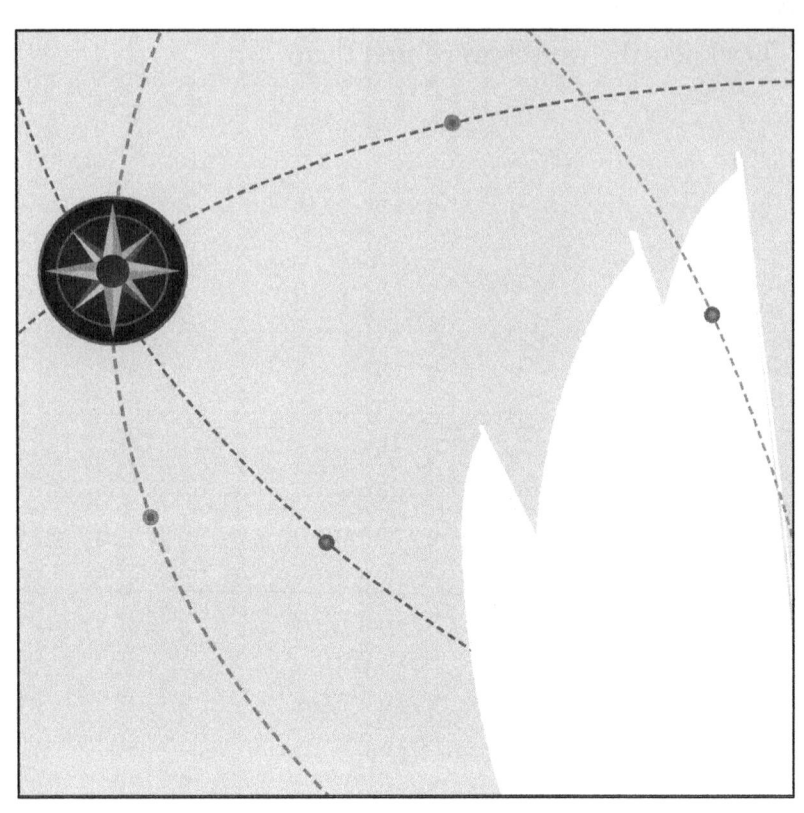

Chapter 14

AS HIS HEARTBEAT FINALLY began to slow down again, Eddie's head began to clear. He lifted his feet and walked around the schooner, scanning every inch of it for significant damages. Then, a thought occurred to him. The book!

Fearing that it had been tossed overboard during the storm, he rushed to the table where he last sat to read it. No trace of it there. Panic immediately set in. What if his father's book, the last connection—and perhaps the strongest connection—that Eddie ever had to his father was floating aimlessly around on the ocean current? Daunted, Eddie slumped down, curling over his bent knees. Then, out of the corner of his eye, he spotted something. The manuscript! It lay limp and damp in a far corner of the deck. It must have been hurled around while the boat was battling against the storm. Eddie leapt at it with both hands out. Grabbing it, he shook off the excess water and scanned the pages. Some of the ink had begun to run, but otherwise the book was in considerably good shape. Breathing a sigh of relief, Eddie brought it back to its original place on the table and turned to head back up to the deck. He let Guinness out, who greeted him by jumping up and placing his paws on Eddie's thighs.

"Let's hope that was the worst of it," Eddie told Guinness, rubbing the dog's face.

The next chapter that Eddie read surprised him. It was different from all previous chapters. Unlike the others, it carried a much more personal tone.

Chapter Five
CHOOSING WHO TO BE

In this chapter, I want to talk about some of the main ideas that I've lived by, ideas that I hope to pass onto my own child. Maybe this book will spark a conversation or two between you and your own children.

Eddie read those words and felt tears forming. There was so much his father had never said to him. There was so much he had never said to his father. He swallowed hard, cringing inwardly at the lost time, the lost chances to communicate.

We live in a world where immoderate behavior is celebrated. It used to be that you'd go out with the fellas after work and maybe have a few pops. A couple of beers, and then you'd call it a night. Or you'd take your girl to the local make-out place, but both of you knew the rules of the game, the limits.

Today, our media culture celebrates the lifestyle of overdoing things—drinking too much, sexual freedom. I'm no prude, but things have gone too far in our world. Don't get me wrong—we've always had heavy drinking. It just seems as though there's a much higher acceptance of overindulgence, not enough moderation.

Today, nobody's speaking out on behalf of the virtues of moderation. Everybody has to be Bill Gates or Warren Buffett or they feel like a failure. Everybody feels as though they have to be a rock star. Talk about how the financial media, especially TV, has created a celebrity system or star system among fund managers, traders, analysts, etc. People are far too interested in developing themselves as a brand instead of providing value and service to the client.

As the concepts of moderation and service have become lost values, the world is too much about "What's in it for me?" Not enough about doing a good turn for humanity, without expecting anything back in return. Everything has been monetized to the point where very few do anything simply because it's the right thing to do.

According to Emerson's Law of Compensation, if you give more than is expected, more will be given to you, either by that particular client or by the universe acting in your favor. Earl Nightingale, the dean of personal development himself, said it best when he said that the universe is impersonal. It doesn't play favorites. Just as there are laws of physics for the physical world, there are certain guidelines for the interpersonal world. Live by them and you win. Ignore them and you pay the price.

I often think about the movie "Pay It Forward" and the ardent message that it sends. When somebody does something nice for you, do something nice for somebody else. Keep it moving forward. It's a simple virtue, but it's a concept that is all but forgotten today, even by people who saw and remember the movie!

In my childhood, I remember a particular lady who was called Aunt Kate by all the children in the playground. She wasn't anyone's aunt, but she loved children. She was there every day in the playground so that the parents could run to the store or do other errands, or just get a break. She never asked for anything—she just enjoyed the fresh air and keeping an eye on the children. That was reward enough for her. Years later, when my business reached a certain level of success, I had the privilege of buying Aunt Kate a condo across from the little park she loved so much. It was the first home she had ever owned. Who was there for you? What can you do for that person? Or what can you do for the people around you, in the spirit of Aunt Kate?

Something else that today's world seems at a loss for is optimism. Why does optimism seem so old-fashioned?

I always saw the glass as half full. While it's much easier to give up and blame everything around you for your shortcomings, it's well worth it to work through your problems and envision a better end in sight. If you think about it, none of the great leaders of the world were cynics. Not Lincoln. Not Washington. Not Churchill or Roosevelt. Not Buddha or Jesus. What cynic or pessimist left a positive mark on society? The cynics and pessimists were the totalitarians—Stalin, Hitler, Mao. These were the people who didn't trust human nature and tried to control it instead of letting it flourish.

Most people live their lives as if they are at the mercy of circumstances, conditions, or whatever they read in the newspaper that morning. We live in a victim-mentality culture. Where did this come from? The biggest problem in America today is the failure of individuals to take responsibility for their choices. Therapy is good so long as it doesn't lead to an abnegation of personal responsibility. Back in the sixties, a comedian named Flip Wilson would say, "The devil made me do it!" Today, everybody sees a thousand devils that made them do...whatever. People make choices, and these choices have ramifications. People need to blame less and take responsibility more.

Before I start sounding like an out-of-touch bore, though, I'd like to make the point that we need to live at cause and not effect. Meaning that while we don't control everything that happens in our lives, like the inattentive driver crossing the line into our lane, we cause and create our lives through our attitudes, our behavior, and our choices. Attitude, behavior, choices—the ABCs of life.

Teach people not to blame others for their situation. I have come across more self-made millionaires with state college educations than all the Ivy League alumni that I know combined. People who see themselves as the cause of their lives instead of being at the mercy of circumstances are able to go out and make great things happen.

I've seen our society change over the last few decades, and not in a positive way. People are too much about themselves and not about others, community, family. I'm guilty of this myself—too much time at work, not enough time at home.

We've all been taught to suppress feelings and instead be rational thinkers. Rationality is good as far as it goes, but at the end of the day, suppression of feelings is unhealthy. It leads us to make poor choices and set misguided priorities.

I can think about a subject all day long, but if I ignore my feelings, I'm never going to get to the heart of the matter. Maybe that's the problem—we're coming too much from our brains and not enough from our hearts. Would we not be a more evolved culture if we all struck a healthy balance between our heads and our hearts?

Is there a common thread here? It's hard to say. Unless it's this: A successful philosophy of life is optimistic, conscious of one's own feelings and the feelings of others, other-oriented as opposed to self-oriented, and looking at the world through eyes of love. I always lived by this philosophy, even before I was conscious of it, and that's the true secret of my success.

While they don't know it, this book is my attempt to make amends to my family for having concentrated too hard on work, missing Little League games, not being around during the holidays. I hope this book can bridge the distance between you and your family as I hope it will between my family and me.

We often find ourselves surrounded by the most magnificent material things in the world, items far beyond the dreams of most people, and we ask the inevitable question: "Is that all there is?" If we are chasing materialistic dreams, then yes, that is all there is. And it's never enough. So we make more money, and wait for a bigger ship to come in, still stuck in the "when/then" mentality—"*When* I reach a certain financial level or attain a certain professional goal, *then* I will be happy." In other words, we postpone joy indefinitely and all too often, die without it.

Obviously this is no way to live.

One of the benefits of growing older is that we learn to place more value on our time than we did when we were young and we thought we had all the time in the world. We no longer wait for happiness. Unfortunately, many of us who have reached "a certain age"—in my case, the mid-fifties—have come to believe that happiness is an illusion, or that happiness, as the expression goes, is like credit—some get it, and some don't. In fact, there is no randomness to happiness. It goes to those who seek it. The reason that most people are unhappy is because they make the mistake of seeking the things they think will make them happy, instead of seeking happiness itself.

I once heard it said that "I used to use people and love things. But then I got wise—now I use things and love people."

How many of us can make a similar claim?

I define success as feeling relatively comfortable most of the time. Perhaps that's not as big, audacious, and outrageous a goal as others may set for themselves. But I speak as one who has achieved most of the goals that mortal men strive for, and I can tell you that all the money in the world doesn't mean a thing when you don't feel comfortable in your own skin. In other words, if you're happy within, you can be happy without, and having everything in the world will not make a dime's bit of difference if you are expecting those outside things to make you happy.

In truth, only you have the power to make yourself happy. They say that you cannot buy happiness. I agree with that, but I will say that you can rent it! The problem is that once the rental period is over, you have to return whatever the thing or person is that brought you that temporary state of happiness. That's not even worth pursuing. What we're all looking for is joy. I define joy as an elevated state of happiness, a state in which we truly find ourselves comfortable in our own skin, able to accept life's blows with equanimity and at the same time able to find happiness and even joy in the everyday.

I can hear you saying, "It's easy for you to say that. You've got everything!"

Fair enough. But I can tell you this: I was just as happy when I didn't have it, and I would still be as happy if I didn't have it. What I have has little to do with who I am. What I've built enables me to go out and get some of the "toys" of life. And those toys are fun! But I know plenty of people who have far, far less than I, and they know a day-to-day happiness that I might never know. Surely Wordsworth understood 21st century life perfectly from his viewpoint in the 19th century when he wrote, "Getting and spending, we lay waste our powers."

So how do you achieve success? The first thing you have to do is define it for yourself. I like boats. You may not. My success might mean little to you if boating isn't your thing. It's not everybody's. You know the expression—"The happiest day of my life is when I bought my boat. The next happiest day was when I sold it."

Take the word boat and replace it with anything that you covet. Maybe it will make you happy. Maybe it won't. But it certainly won't make everyone on the planet happy. That's why you have to define your own success in your own terms. What is it? And why is it so? Again, remember that the enemy in life is not failure, because failure is simply a piece of information that points you toward a better path. The real enemy is drift, and drift occurs when we don't have a clear goal in mind, a star to steer by. So you must first get clear about what you want. Fantasize about it, if you will. I'd be lying to you if I didn't fantasize about running my own highly successful financial services firm. That was my goal from the time I first heard of such things: Make lots of money, be my own boss.

Everyone's different. You must have your own clearly defined sense of success, and you must fantasize about it, make it real in your subconscious mind, which cannot tell the difference between what is real and what you say is real. This is how you bring something from the possible into the actual, and this is what you must do.

You must relinquish your sense of control over the process by which you will achieve your goal. Indeed, control is an illusion. We control nothing in life. Any of us could die at any moment, and there goes all our illusory control. Money, property, prestige—none of these things kept Lady Di or J.F.K., Jr. from their sudden demise, and if their elevated status in society could not protect them, then obviously nothing can protect the rest of us. But you don't need protection, and you don't need control. Indeed, to seek to control the means by which your goal is brought to life is to choke off all possibilities that have not already come to your mind. I don't advise that, as you can imagine. Instead, relinquish control. Let go. Let the universal energy find the means for your goal to come to existence and at the same time, learn to appreciate what you already have.

The law of appreciation is one of the unbreakable tenets by which the universe grants or fails to grant wishes. A father looks at his toddler son and says, "Why should I give you another toy? You don't even appreciate the one I gave you last time." Appreciate what you have—it's a signal to the universe that you will appreciate and take good care of whatever comes next into your life. Remember that we don't really keep anything forever, because we don't last forever. If anything, we are temporary stewards of whatever good fortune comes our way. Nothing is forever, including ownership. So see if you can appreciate what you have now, because that is a clear signal to the universe that you are ready to have—and appreciate—even more.

The next step is simply to be the person who would be

appropriate to do the kinds of things that would generate the kind of income or possessions or other goals that you seek. In the West, we get it backwards. We think life is a game of "have, do, be." Life is truly a game of "be, do, have."

Are you operating the law of attraction to your benefit? Are you being the kind of person who others would like to work with, love, or spend time with? Or are you taking as your role model the kind of negative people who are out there in abundance, and who appear to have it all because they have external wealth but in fact have nothing because they have no internal happiness?

So first you must **be** the kind of person you think you would **be**, if you got to **do** all the things you wanted to **do**, and **have** all the things that you wanted to **have**. And if you are that positive person, universal energy will make opportunities available to you to do the things that you want to do—and as a result, you'll get the things that you want to "have." Be, do, have.

Reverse the West's pattern and you can reverse the course in your life. Choose your own direction. Then consciously steer your life towards it.

Takeaway #1: When somebody does something nice to you, do something nice for somebody else. Few things in life are as gratifying as being on the giving end of a random act of kindness. By circulating positive energy, we surround ourselves with it.

Takeaway #2: Everyone's different. You must have your own clearly defined sense of success, and you must fantasize about it, make it real in your subconscious mind, which cannot tell the difference between what is real and what you say is real. This is how you bring something from the possible into the actual.

Takeaway #3: Be. Do. Have. First, **be** the person you envision yourself to be. Take the necessary actions and **do** what is necessary to be that person. These actions will then guide you to the things you want to **have**.

Who do you want to be? What do you have to do in order to be that person? Find these answers, and you will have it! Your subconscious mind cannot separate what you wish you had and what you are. If you always "want" something, you will spend your life "wanting" it. Instead, have it. For example, if your desired weight is 175 pounds, say that you are 175 pounds—not that you want it to be so. If you desire to secure the title of top salesperson, then state that you are exactly that. Write down who you choose to be. And then state what you need to do to achieve it. Next, **take action**. You will be amazed at what will begin to manifest in your life if you follow this simple formula.

Action Step 7:

Who do you want to be?
    1. I AM _____
    2. I AM _____
    3. I AM _____

What do you want to do?
    1. _____
    2. _____
    3. _____

What do you want to have?
    1. _____
    2. _____
    3. _____

Are you willing to change your life in order to accomplish these? Circle those items above that you will commit to.

What actions are necessary in order to move directionally toward the ones you circled?

_____
_____
_____
_____

Now execute your plan!

Chapter Six
THE EGO

Accepting the status quo in our society is "normal." I've heard over and over again from people that they just want to be "normal." I would never want to be normal! Not in this society! In our society, if we define normal as "being like everyone else," then normal is dysfunctional. Normal is often unhappy, sometimes angry, and usually unfulfilled. I would never want to be normal, because unfortunately, those negative terms represent the norms of attitudes and behavior in our society. I don't want to be normal—I want to be healthy...and I want to be happy. And because I have made a study of how to attain happiness—a study that I am summarizing in these pages—I have in fact attained it. And that is why I am sharing these thoughts with you.

So what truly keeps you from being happy? In a word: Ego. Ego stands for Edging God Out. Ego would have you believe that you don't need any help, you can do everything all by yourself. Ego wants to keep you from enjoying the present moment. Ego tells you that you will be happy one day, but you do not have to be happy now. Ego tells you that you must remain mired in the past or projecting into the future, thinking about, dwelling on, stuck in old situations, or worrying about the myriad of things that could go wrong. What if instead we realized that nothing can be done about past or future at this point? Present moment is the place that the most spiritually advanced among us spend the bulk of their existence. The place where true happiness exists is now. It is the only time that exists. No one has ever done anything in the past or future—they did it in their now. Even Einstein argued that this concept we view as time which we use to measure past and future is simply an illusion created by the velocity at which we (the Earth) are moving through space.

This presence we are calling universal energy can only be found in the moment of now, and ego wants to take you out of the present and put you into an uncomfortable past or an uncertain future. In the moment, you have no problems. In the moment, all is well. And yet, we spend so much of our time in fear or in resentment, in the future or in the past. Your job is to make a comfortable nest of the present moment, and to keep your ego from pulling you out of the present and away from this universal energy. We are prisoners of our ego all too often because we live in a world of negativity. Our advertising culture constantly reminds us of the things that we don't have and the things that we think we must have. Most people have internal dialogues that tend toward the negative. We are all too often surrounded, at work, and even at home, by people with negative attitudes about life. People see themselves as victims, instead of recognizing the power they have to positively transform their lives and the lives of those around them.

We live marinated in judgment—and by judgment I mean condemnation of the gift of life and everything positive that we could be enjoying. We constantly evaluate others based on our societal norms. We create labels for them if they don't match our ideals. We allow these judgments to effect the way we think, act, and treat others. We fail to forgive others or ourselves for errors in judgment and mistakes, expecting perfection from imperfect beings and staying miserable because we fail to forgive. Thus we find ourselves stuck in fear. What if we simply stopped judging? Started going through life accepting things as they are? Conflicts would fall away. We couldn't complain for without judgment there is nothing to complain about. Think about how much happiness could be added to our lives if we just stopped judging.

All these mental constructs we create for ourselves through judgment or projection into the past or future create fear. In modern times we refer to it as "stress." Stress isn't the enemy. Stress is usually a misnomer. What we think is stress is actually our inability to be happy, and typically our inability to be happy is a function of our willingness to let our egos dictate how we should be, whom we should be, and what we should do. Obviously you can see that this is a nonsensical way of life. We take ourselves too seriously. We think we are the masters of the universe, especially if we get a little jingle in our pockets! In fact, we are not masters but servants. We are here to serve each other. I have found the most joyous among us are those that serve others. Pleasure may come from getting and spending, but not true happiness. And yet, as a human race, we are utterly overconfident. All you have to do is look back at any century or even any decade of human history to recognize just how fallacious and suicidal our overconfidence really is.

I want you to wake up to true reality. I want you to see life as a dream instead of a nightmare or a struggle. It's your life. What will you create? What fears are holding you back from the dreams of your life?

Takeaway #1: Do not strive for normalcy. Instead, opt to achieve happiness and joy.

Takeaway #2: Ego often blocks us from achieving what we want out of life by distracting us from the existence of happiness in the present moment.

Takeaway #3: From Ego comes victimhood and judgment. The victim is absorbed in the past. He can't move forward because he has relinquished his energy. The judge is mired in negativity because no one can live up to his expectations. Resist the impulse to blame and complain. Accept responsibility for everything that happens to you, and you take control of the energy of your existence. The blaming, complaining, and victimhood all fall away.

Takeaway #4: We spend considerable time spinning worst case scenarios about particular events in our minds. We mire in these scenarios over and over again. Rarely does the worst case ever truly happen. Ask yourself, what would happen if you lived a truly stress-free life by functioning without fear?

Remember, 95% of what we worry about never comes to be.

My hope for your outcome of the forthcoming action step, is the realization that you can break the stress down to its very drivers, see them for what they are, and allow those underlying fears to fall away.

Action Step 8:

Name the 3 biggest issues that contribute to stress in your life?

    1. _____
    2. _____
    3. _____

If these fears/stressors play out what is the worst case scenario for each?

    1. _____
    2. _____
    3. _____

If that scenario were to happen what opportunity might it present?

    1. _____
    2. _____
    3. _____

How would your existence be altered by each worst case scenario?

    1. _____
    2. _____
    3. _____

What is the realistic probability of each scenario occurring?

    1. _____
    2. _____
    3. _____

Action Step 8 (Cont'd):

If each issue that you are experiencing fear/stress over doesn't ever come to fruition, then what?

1. _____
2. _____
3. _____

Do you have control over the issue?

1. _____
2. _____
3. _____

If yes, what can you do to influence a favorable outcome? What is stopping you from doing it now?

1. _____
2. _____
3. _____

If no, does it serve you to worry about that which you cannot control? Imagine the most optimum outcome. See it clearly in your mind. Feel what it would be like if this outcome played out. Replay that feeling in your mind and see it or something better coming to be.

Chapter Seven
THE PRESENT MOMENT

Let's say you were actually playing a video game called "Nothing Matters"—and that aside from hurting other people, you had absolute freedom to fashion your life as you saw it? Would that change things? Would that make you happier? Would that create an opening for happiness to enter your life?

A four-year-old looks at life and smiles because he experiences life in the moment, secure in the knowledge of abundance and fearlessness. A forty-year-old looks at life, often with despair. "I haven't made enough money. Time is running out. I'm losing my looks." No wonder everybody's so unhappy.

Again, how do you achieve this? It's not as hard as it seems. Live in the now. Live in the moment. Don't let your ego take you out of it. Decide on the result you're looking for; adjust your thought and action to that course; maintain the discipline to see it through; and you will have a more desirous outcome.

Takeaway #1: Be in the now. Stop worrying about yesterday. It's over. Stop fretting about tomorrow. It hasn't happened yet. Give your energy and attention to exactly what you are engaged in at that time, whether it is an important business meeting, your kid's sports game, or that conversation with your spouse.

Takeaway #2: Optimism is not outdated. Be joyful and you will be surrounded by it.

Takeaway #3: Be honest with yourself about the things you want—or don't want—in your life. Without recognizing why you want something, you will rarely get it.

Final Action Step:

Write your life's description by combining what you've learned from all the action steps you've done.

- Life Balance (p. 70)
- Surrounding yourself with positive influences (p. 87, 89)
- Your desires (p. 105)
- Your life's fulfillment (p. 111-112)
- Who you want to be (p. 130)
- Dissolution of irrational fears (p. 135-136)

Your description should provide a vivid picture of your desired life situation. Now close your eyes and fantasize about this life. Be in the moment with as much detail as your imagination can provide. What does it feel like? Notice the sensation in your stomach and chest. Play this over and over again in your mind and allow the feeling to flow through you. That feeling is the energy. Use whatever means you can to keep this feeling with you and revert back to this state whenever you can. The more you are able to attain this energetic state the higher the probability it becomes your reality.

_____
_____
_____
_____
_____

Chapter 15

WITH THAT THE BOOK ended—far too abruptly for Eddie, who sat astonished. He sat for a while, letting his brain soak in his father's words. Why is it that he is only now finding out what message his father wanted to leave behind? Why didn't his father ever try sitting him down and telling Eddie himself? Questions littered Eddie's mind. He decided to get up and walk around.

As he stood, a piece of paper fell loose from the manuscript. Afraid that the book had started to fall to pieces, Eddie reached for it. Examining it, he realized that this page was different from all the others. Instead of printed text, the page was handwritten. It was his father's handwriting. It seemed to be a full sheet of other lessons and takeaways. Perhaps they were his father's notes. Sentences were crossed out, then re-written.

> Decide how you want your life to be with as much clarity as possible. This constitutes your thoughts, which will create the energy pattern.

> Experience/fantasize the feeling of what it would be like to live this desired life. The feeling

directs the energy, so it is important that you tune your feelings to your desires.

> Decide what action(s) you can take to bring your intended desire(s) closer to fruition. Break down your action steps into time increments (daily, weekly, monthly, yearly, quarterly, and annually).

> Build daily routines around performing your action steps. It is much easier and requires less energy to establish actions into routines.

> Seek to eliminate any external influences that negatively affect your flow toward your desires.

> Obstacles will always arise just as traffic and highway construction will affect a road trip across the country. As you encounter obstacles, think back to a time in your life when you were successful in a similar endeavor. Begin operating from that feeling of success. That sets your energy in a positive direction. Trust that the process works and you will reach your destination, which in this case is the fulfillment of your desire.

> Mental discipline is the key to success. Know that you have the ability to control your thoughts. The more practice you put into controlling your mind, the more proficient you will become. This will dramatically reduce the time it takes to reach your desires.

They seemed like disconnected thoughts, nothing like the eloquent flow of life advice that poured through the manuscript he had just read. Perhaps they were ideas that his dad was brainstorming along the way. Eager to find an answer, Eddie re-read the page as if it would help him uncover the mystery. Then, he flipped the page over and saw a note that made his heart sink right to his feet.

❂ ❂ ❂

To Whom It May Concern,

Storm brewing, sails torn, and ship partially flooded. Unlikely that I will make it back to land. Opposite page are thoughts to be included in book. Please get this manuscript to my son, Edward Noonan, Jr., if found.

Gratefully,
Ned Noonan

❂ ❂ ❂

It was finally clear to him. His father had thought himself close to the end during a terrible storm and wrote out this note to whoever came across the book, in case he never made it. Kathy had found the manuscript copy in a plastic bag, meant to protect the book from the forces of nature.

He finally realized what his father's intentions were, despite his rigid, businesslike facade. The entire time, he had meant the contents of this book to be for Eddie. He had loved and wanted the best for his family, for him. He couldn't help but feel overwhelmed that his father had written the manuscript to pass on his deepest values not only to his readers but also to him. He held the manuscript, put his head down, and sobbed quietly so that Kathy wouldn't hear him.

Dad, he thought. *It's not your fault. It's mine.*

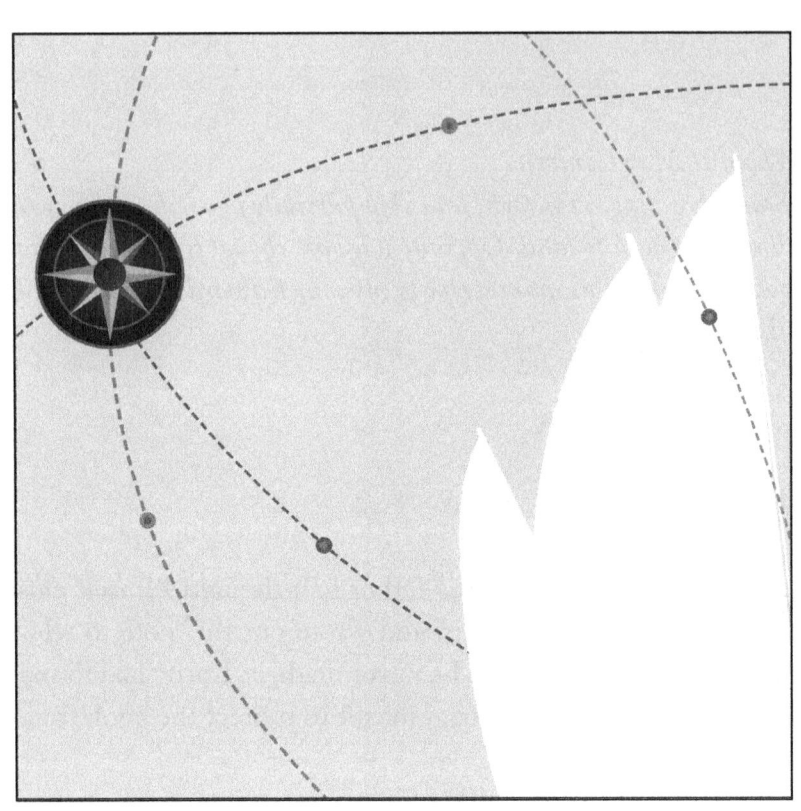

Chapter 16

THE STORM HAD PASSED, but not their exhaustion or the damage to the *Maximum Liquidity*. The boat looked thrashed. Water was everywhere. The broken mast that Eddie had rigged gave the boat an almost comical look. Eddie and Kathy both stared at it with haggard, wasted expressions on their faces, as if to say, "How did that thing stay in place?" Neither knew.

They barely had any energy to talk, or even to sit up straight. They both sat slumped in the helm, feeling barely alive. Weather conditions had returned to something close to normal: gray skies and a slightly choppy sea, but mercifully, no more rain or wind.

"I half expect a dove with an olive branch in its mouth to appear any time now," Kathy finally said, and the comment broke the tension.

Eddie laughed.

"Or a bagel with butter," Eddie said. "Wouldn't it be great if a dove showed up with a bagel with butter?"

"Why a bagel with butter?" Kathy asked.

Eddie shrugged. "It's what I used to have for breakfast before I went into work," he said.

"I just got a taste for one right now."

"That's the scariest thing I've ever been through in my whole life," Kathy said.

Eddie nodded. "Worst storm I've ever seen," he said. "Let alone sailed through. I just kept thinking that this had to be the same kind of storm my father went through. Unfortunately, he didn't have anybody to hold the wheel."

They both fell silent now, contemplating Ned's fate.

"Are you saying," Kathy began slowly, "that my being here… made a difference?"

"You can't hold a boat steady and rig a mast at the same time," Eddie said. "You can try to do one or the other. But in a storm like that, good luck to you."

"Your father would have been proud of you," Kathy said.

"My father would have been proud of you," Eddie replied, and their eyes met.

"So," Kathy said, sitting up in her chair, "now what? What's our plan? Stay on the same route? Turn around?"

"I hadn't really thought about it," Eddie said, "to be honest. But I think it's really your call."

"My call?" Kathy asked, surprised. "I'm just a stowaway."

Eddie shook his head. "Not anymore," he said. "You're co-captain. I really don't believe I would have survived this without you."

"Not bad for a girl's first time on the water," Kathy said, grinning. "Tell me sailing isn't always like this."

Eddie nodded. "Sailing isn't always like this," he said. "Usually it's a lot smoother. Usually, you don't almost die in gale force winds."

"Glad to hear that," Kathy said. "I'd hate to think that everybody who owned a boat was either a masochist or totally suicidal."

"That's a once-in-a-lifetime storm," Eddie said. "Either you don't take your boat out if you know the conditions are going to be that way, or you don't survive. Either way, it's once in a lifetime."

"So how did we end up in it, anyway?" Kathy asked.

"You can't predict everything," Eddie admitted. "There are a lot of storms that you can predict and either steer around or delay your trip. This one was a surprise."

"Just like life," Kathy said.

Eddie thought for a moment. He nodded. "Just like life," he agreed.

Kathy smiled.

"This is probably where he died," Eddie said. "And this is probably how he died, in a storm just like this."

They remained silent for a while as the prow of the boat cut through waves that were a small fraction of what had been threatening the vessel and its occupants only hours earlier.

"Would it be too egotistical," Eddie began slowly, looking directly at Kathy, "for me to say that my father had an audience of one in mind—me? Now that I read the manuscript, it served its purpose?"

Kathy stared off at the horizon, visible once again, as the sky continued to lighten.

"Makes sense to me," she said quietly. "I'm sure your father would have liked it to be a big bestseller. But I think it's more important that he reached his intended audience."

"So what do you want to do?" Eddie asked. "I'm sure if we turned around now, we could eventually make landfall somewhere in Nova Scotia. And then you could catch a flight back to Boston."

Kathy frowned. "What would your father say?" she asked with mild disapproval in her voice. "Energy in life is much like the current and weather on the sea, you can't control it, but you must accept what is and navigate through it. The whole point of your father's book is that you don't let storms or any other obstacle keep you from your destination. At least, once you have a destination. And we do."

"But I wouldn't want to put you through another storm like that," Eddie said. "And you never know what you're going to get out there. I never knew we'd get this one."

"Maybe I nearly died," Kathy said, "but since the first time I started in law school, I've really felt alive. I'm game."

"I just don't know about that mast," Eddie said. "I don't know if it's strong enough."

"I don't really know how to answer that," Kathy said, studying it. "But it looks secure enough. And as long as we don't have another storm like that, we could probably get it repaired once we get to Ireland."

Eddie laughed. "With what money?" he asked.

"I can wait tables, and you can tend bar," Kathy told him, her grin widening. "We'll make enough money to get the boat fixed and go home."

"Maybe we'll never go home," Eddie said. "Maybe Ireland will be home."

Kathy thought for a moment.

"I think your father would be very proud of you right now," Kathy said. "You know what you need to do for yourself right now. You're open to new possibilities. You've got good energy. I think your father would be very proud of you right now."

"Proud of us," Eddie said. He was about to reach over and kiss her, when suddenly one last giant wave came out of nowhere and swamped the boat. It soaked them all over again, and they both started to laugh.

"I think your father sent that wave," Kathy said, after they had wiped the water from their faces. "Telling us to stick to business."

"That sounds like my father," Eddie admitted. "He always thought I was kind of a goof-off."

"Not anymore," Kathy said.

Eddie weighed her words. And he had to agree.

"Not anymore," he said contentedly.

"Maybe your real journey," Kathy mused, "is to finish your father's book. Create a message to share with the world."

"How do I even figure out where to start?" Eddie asked.

"Only you can figure that out. Your dad's trip to Ireland wasn't finished and neither was his book. Maybe you're supposed to complete both."

He felt a chill. He knew she was right. He was meant to complete not just his father's journey but his father's message as well.

"I'm not exactly a role model for humanity," he said meekly.

"You saved my life," Kathy said. "That's a start."

Eddie thought about her words.

"Maybe there's something more to me than just a trust fund baby who can sail."

"I think that's exactly what we're learning," Kathy said, giving him a warm smile.

Eddie returned the smile, checked the navigation equipment, and steered the *Maximum Liquidity* to its destination.

Ireland.

THE END

NOTES:

NOTES:

CPSIA information can be obtained at www.ICGtesting.com
Printed in the USA
LVOW02*1614030614

388425LV00001B/1/P